Foreign Direct Investment in Southeast Asia

The **Institute of Southeast Asian Studies** (ISEAS) was established as an autonomous organization in 1968. It is a regional research centre for scholars and other specialists concerned with modern Southeast Asia, particularly the many-faceted problems of stability and security, economic development, and political and social change.

The Institute is governed by a twenty-two-member Board of Trustees comprising nominees from the Singapore Government, the National University of Singapore, the various Chambers of Commerce, and professional and civic organizations. A ten-man Executive Committee oversees day-to-day operations; it is chaired by the Director, the Institute's chief academic and administrative officer.

The **ASEAN Economic Research Unit** (AERU) is an integral part of the Institute, coming under the overall supervision of the Director who is also the Chairman of its Management Committee. The Unit was formed in 1979 in response to the need to deepen understanding of economic change and political developments in ASEAN. A Regional Advisory Committee, consisting of a senior economist from each of the ASEAN countries, guides the work of the Unit.

ISEAS Current Economic Affairs Series

Foreign Direct Investment in Southeast Asia

Differential Impacts

Maxwell J. Fry
University of Birmingham

ASEAN Economic Research Unit
INSTITUTE OF SOUTHEAST ASIAN STUDIES

Published by
Institute of Southeast Asian Studies
Heng Mui Keng Terrace
Pasir Panjang Road
Singapore 0511

Cataloguing in Publication Data

Fry, Maxwell J.
Foreign direct investment in Southeast Asia : differential impacts.
(ISEAS current economic affairs series)
1. Investments, Foreign — Southeast Asia.
I. Title.
II. Series.
HG5770.5 A3F94 1993 sls93-79784

ISBN 981-3016-72-8
ISSN 0218-2114

The responsibility for facts and opinions in this publication rests exclusively with the author and his interpretations do not necessarily reflect the views or the policy of the Institute or its supporters.

Printed in Singapore by Prime Packaging Industries Pte. Ltd.

Dedicated to the memory of
Professor K.S. Sandhu
Director of ISEAS, 1972–1992

Contents

Tables

Figures

Acknowledgements

My thanks go to Jagdish Bhagwati, Maja Bresslauer, Richard Caves, Stijn Claessens, Michael Dooley, Persa Economou, Antonio Estache, John Fender, Jeffrey Frankel, Ann Harrison, Ronald Johannes, Kwang Jun, Osamu Kawaguchi, Homi Kharas, Danny Leipziger, Jaime de Melo, Chris Milner, John Morris, Peng Wen-Sheng, Eric Pentecost, Guy Pfeffermann, Andrzej Raczko, James Tybout, Alan Winters, and seminar participants at the Institute of Southeast Asian Studies, the University of Birmingham, Keele University, Loughborough University, and the National University of Singapore for their comments and help. This book was written while I was a senior fellow in international banking and finance at the Institute of Southeast Asian Studies in Singapore. I am most grateful to the Institute for its generous hospitality and for enabling me to visit the Southeast Asian countries analysed in this study. The econometric work in this book was carried out for the International Department of the World Bank under the World Bank's Research Support Budget RPO 678–15; my thanks also go to the World Bank for its support. The views expressed in this book do not necessarily reflect those of the World Bank, its Board of Directors, its management, or any of its member countries. *MicroTSP*, version 7.0, was used for all graphics and regressions presented here.

1 Introduction

THE BALANCE-OF-PAYMENTS ACCOUNTS show that a current account deficit is financed by capital inflows or decreases in official reserves. One way of presenting this identity is:[1]

$$CA + KA \equiv \Delta R, \tag{1}$$

where CA is the current account, KA is the capital account, and ΔR is the change in official reserves. As an item in the balance-of-payments accounts, foreign direct investment (FDI) is one of several capital flows. Other things equal, therefore, an increase in FDI increases capital inflows. If the change in official reserves is unaffected, the increased capital inflow is matched by a smaller current account surplus or a larger current account deficit.

The current account itself can be defined as the difference between national saving S and domestic investment I:

$$CA \equiv S - I. \tag{2}$$

The most obvious link between FDI and the current account in equation 2 is through domestic investment. If FDI finances additional capital formation in the host country, it raises domestic investment I. Equation 2 shows that this worsens the current account as required by equation 1.

[1] This identity ignores errors and omissions.

The current account can also be defined as the difference between exports of goods and services X plus net factor income from abroad NFI and imports of goods and services IM:

$$CA \equiv X + NFI - IM. \qquad (3)$$

If FDI increases capital formation in the host country, the increased investment could involve increased imports of raw materials or capital equipment. Alternatively, it could reduce exports by diverting them into the additional investment. In either case, the current account must deteriorate in equation 3 by exactly the same amount as it does in equations 1 and 2.

If FDI finances additional capital formation, equation 2 demonstrates that the current account deteriorates to the same extent that FDI increases capital inflows. In such case, FDI cannot provide additional foreign exchange to finance a pre-existing current account deficit. The extra foreign exchange is entirely absorbed in financing a larger current account deficit.

However, an increase in FDI could provide additional finance for the balance of payments if it failed to result in additional capital formation in the host country. In undertaking any analysis of FDI, one must recognise that FDI data record financial flows which may or may not correspond to changes in capital formation. Whether or not they do depends on the extents of crowding out of domestically financed investment and substitutability of this type of financial flow for other types of financial flows.

Suppose that FDI capital inflows were used for new capital formation. If this capital formation would have taken place in any event or if this capital formation deters an equal amount of domestically financed investment in other projects, then total domestic investment I remains unchanged. In such case, FDI does not affect the current account unless it changes the level of national saving. If the current account and the change in official reserves remain the same, this FDI becomes one of the sources of finance for the pre-existing current account deficit.

An inflow of FDI also provides balance-of-payments financing if it is not used for new capital formation. For example, privatization programmes in a number of countries have produced capital inflows in the form of FDI. The privatization has resulted in foreign ownership of an existing company and its capital assets, but not necessarily in any new capital formation. Typically, a capital inflow used to acquire ownership of an existing firm is recorded as FDI if it achieves ownership of 10 per cent or more in the company. Again, this FDI is not accompanied by additional capital formation and so does not increase the current account deficit. It does, therefore, provide additional or alternative balance-of-payments financing.

Some of the literature on FDI suggests that FDI can serve two purposes, namely, increase investment and relieve foreign exchange shortages. For example, Cockcroft and Riddell note:

> Two of the principal factors inhibiting higher levels of economic growth in Sub-Saharan Africa in the 1990s are low levels of investment and foreign exchange shortages. The first attraction of foreign investment lies in its potential to address both these constraints. (1991, p. 3)

Unless it affects national saving, however, FDI can increase domestic investment, or it can provide additional financing for a pre-existing current account deficit, or it can achieve some combination of the two. However, the linear combination of these two effects must always sum to one.

In the more aggregated balance-of-payments accounts, such as those presented in *International Financial Statistics* that are used in this study, FDI is recorded as a net inflow of capital. It is net in two senses: first, it nets out capital outflows; second, it nets out profit repatriation. Hence, two countries with similar FDI could experience different changes in foreign ownership. In one country, there might be no FDI outflow nor any repatriated profits. Hence, US$1 million FDI implies a transfer of US$1 million of foreign capital into ownership of companies in the host company. In another country, however, a US$3 million FDI inflow and US$2 million FDI outflow would imply a much larger increase in foreign ownership despite the same net flow of FDI.

In any event, foreign control over a company does not require 100 per cent foreign ownership. Furthermore, 100 per cent foreign ownership can be achieved without 100 per cent foreign equity financing; funds can be borrowed in the host country to finance part of the acquisition or establishment of a company. Hence, the recorded net inflow of FDI may bear little or no relation to the extent of foreign control or foreign production in the economy. Were one investigating the hypothesis that FDI produced more or less productive projects than domestically financed investment, one would examine data on individual companies that could be classified as foreign or domestically owned. On the other hand, if one wishes to address the question of the macroeconomic impact of FDI across a number of countries, aggregate FDI flow data have to be used.

Over the past decade, many developing countries have taken a fresh look at their policies towards FDI. Since 1982, foreign capital inflows to developing countries have declined and world real interest rates have increased. It is against this background that FDI has been viewed by some as a panacea for declining domestic investment and higher costs of borrowing abroad. The empirical evidence provides no support for such euphoria.

Foreign direct investment appears attractive because it involves a risk-sharing relationship with investors from the home country. Such risk-sharing does not exist in the formal contractual arrangements for foreign loans. Foreign direct investment appears particularly attractive when existing stocks are low. Low stocks of foreign-owned capital imply low flows of repatriated profits. Over time, however, success in attracting FDI will increase this counterflow, which could exceed the alternative flow of interest payments in the longer run. Clearly, therefore, the question of the cost of FDI to reduce risk must be addressed in any evaluation of the benefits to be derived from substituting FDI for foreign borrowing.

Analysis of FDI falls roughly into four categories: (a) descriptive studies in which long lists of government incentives and disincentives are compiled and discussed;[2] (b) macroeconomic studies

---

[2]Guisinger (1986) lists sixty-four types of government incentives and disincentives affecting FDI. The Organisation for Economic Co-operation and Development (1989, pp. 21–25) provides another long list.

of the determinants of aggregate FDI; (c) macroeconomic analysis of the effects of FDI and other capital inflows on the rate of economic growth; (d) microeconomic studies of the effects of FDI in specific industries that examine the productivity or efficiency of FDI compared with domestically financed investment. The present study falls into the third category of FDI studies in that it examines the effects of FDI within a macroeconomic framework.

The next chapter examines the global trends in FDI. Chapter 3 then addresses the question of whether FDI to a sample of sixteen developing countries provided additional foreign exchange for balance-of-payments support. In Chapter 4, I develop a five-equation macroeconomic model with which to examine the effects of FDI on domestic investment, national saving, exports, imports, and the rate of economic growth. I present the estimates of this model in Chapter 5.

By analysing FDI in a macroeconomic framework, this study throws new light on various channels through which FDI influences saving, investment, growth, and the balance of payments on current account. The finding that FDI has differential impacts in a sample of five Southeast Asian and eleven other developing countries leads to several policy conclusions.[3] First, if FDI is attracted for privatization or debt-equity swap programmes, it may provide additional or alternative balance-of-payments support, but it will not accelerate capital formation or economic growth. Second, in the presence of financial and trade distortions, FDI can remove from the host country more than it contributes. In other words, it can be immiserizing. Third, the most efficacious way of encouraging FDI is to implement policies that generally improve the investment climate. Where domestically financed investment is booming, FDI will seek to participate. Finally, maximum benefit from FDI can be achieved in open economies that are free of domestic distortions such as financial repression and trade controls.

---

[3]In this study, the developing market economies of Southeast Asia refer to Indonesia, Korea, Malaysia, the Philippines, and Thailand. Throughout this book, Korea refers to the Republic of Korea, commonly known as South Korea.

2 Global Trends and Foreign Direct Investment Flows to Southeast Asian Developing Economies

FOREIGN CAPITAL INFLOWS to developing countries constitute part of the world's saving. Over the past two decades, world saving as a proportion of world income has fallen. A comparison of the periods 1968–81 and 1982–88 illustrates this worldwide decline in saving ratios (Aghevli et al. 1990, pp. 9 and 36–37): saving in developed countries has fallen from 25 to 20 per cent of GNP and developing country saving has fallen from 25 to 22 per cent of GNP. One important reason for the worldwide decline in saving is rising government deficits: up from 2.9 per cent in the period 1972–80 to 4.5 per cent in the period 1981–88 (*International Financial Statistics Yearbook* [1988, p. 156; 1991, p. 156]).

The decline in world saving implies that not every country can maintain its level of domestic investment by increasing foreign capital inflows. Overall, the decline in saving has to be matched by an equal decline in investment. In fact, saving and investment ratios have fallen in all geographical regions of the world since 1982, but least in developing countries of Asia and the Pacific. As world saving has shrunk, so the world real interest rate has risen from 1.5 per cent during the period 1970–80 to 4.8 per cent in the period 1981–91. With no signs of a reversal in the declining trend in global saving and the immediate saving-reducing impacts of the war in the Gulf, reunification of Germany, reconstruction of Eastern Europe, and deliberate current account-reduction policies being implemented by Japan, Korea, and Taiwan, the costs of foreign borrowing can be expected to rise still higher in the 1990s.

The decline in foreign capital inflows to developing countries has necessitated structural adjustment in the form of an increase in export earnings or a reduction in import expenditure. The national accounting identities imply that the adjustment has to raise national saving or reduce domestic investment. To maintain or increase rates of economic growth, the adjustment must be in the form of increased exports and increased national saving. Import compression and reduced domestic investment inevitably lower growth rates. However, as Faini and de Melo note, "with the significant exception of East Asian countries, adjustment was achieved by cutting investment rather than increasing saving" (1990, p. 492). The inevitable effect has been sharp reductions in rates of growth in all parts of the developing world, again with the exception of Asia and the Pacific.

It is against this background that FDI has appeared increasingly attractive to developing countries facing declining domestic investment and higher costs of foreign borrowing. Globally, FDI has increased dramatically over the past decade. However, most of this increase has occurred in the industrial countries. In the developing countries, FDI has been heavily concentrated among a small number of countries. Indeed, Table 1 shows that over 90 per cent of FDI inflows to developing countries in 1990 was received by only eighteen countries. Half of this total flowed to eight Southeast Asian developing market economies (Hong Kong, Indonesia, Korea, Malaysia, Philippines, Singapore, Taiwan, and Thailand). Given that neither Korea nor Taiwan has shown strong interest in attracting FDI, it may seem surprising that these economies feature in Table 1. The explanation lies in their superlative investment climates (Fry 1991).

Although the Southeast Asian developing economies pursue export-oriented development policies, their policies towards capital account liberalization differ substantially. Hong Kong, Singapore, and Malaysia have open capital accounts, while Korea and

TABLE 1
Foreign Direct Investment Inflows, 1990

Country	US$ millions
Industrial countries	151,970
Developing countries	32,473
Argentina	2,036
Bermuda	819
Brazil	2,118
Chile	595
China	3,489
Colombia	501
Egypt	947
Hong Kong	783
Indonesia	964
Korea	715
Malaysia	2,902
Mexico	2,632
Nigeria	588
Philippines	530
Saudi Arabia	572
Singapore	4,808
Taiwan	1,330
Thailand	2,376
Turkey	697
Venezuela	451

Source: United Nations, *World Investment Report 1992: Transnational Corporations as Engines of Growth* (1992), annex table 1, pp. 312–16.

Taiwan have liberalized slowly and reluctantly. Nevertheless, Hill detects a common trend:

> A key feature of East Asia has been an increasingly open and receptive policy environment during the 1980s for a variety of reasons: the need to recycle trade surpluses (in Korea and Taiwan); greater confidence in the competitive capacities of domestic business groups (these two states plus Thailand); economic imperatives, such as a deteriorating current account for all or part of the decade (Indonesia, Malaysia, the Philippines); and a perception that FDI may be preferable to local non-indigenous investment (as in Malaysia). (1990, p. 24)

Less liberal capital account policies in Korea and Taiwan appear not to have been costly in terms of foregone growth. Indeed, Dornbusch and Park conclude:

> The overriding characteristic of private capital flows, without much exaggeration, is that capital tends to come when it is unnecessary and leave when it is least convenient. As a result it tends to increase the variability of real exchange rates and introduces avoidable macroeconomic instability. One cannot escape the impression that Korea, under the impact of abundant external capital, might lose its competitive exchange rate, overborrow, and ultimately become once again a problem debtor. Korea's investment rate is more than 30 percent of GNP. There is little to suggest that capital imports are necessary because capital is in short supply. (1987, pp. 432–33)

The question which I now address is whether FDI flows to developing countries have provided additional balance-of-payments financing.

3 Does Foreign Direct Investment Provide More Balance-of-Payments Financing?

As the global supply of capital has dwindled, some have seen FDI as a potential additional source of finance for the balance of payments. Using Meade's (1951) distinction between autonomous and accommodating capital flows, Turner (1991, pp. 91–95) addresses the question of whether or not net FDI inflows are accommodating and hence constitute additional financing for the balance of payments by regressing components of the capital account on the current account financing requirement (both in first differences) for some countries of the Organisation for Economic Co-operation and Development (OECD). The estimated equation takes the form:

$$\Delta KF_i = a_0 + a_1 \Delta KFR, \tag{4}$$

where ΔKF_i is the year-on-year change in the net capital flow item expressed as a percentage of GNP and ΔKFR is the year-on-year change in the current account minus the official settlements balance also expressed as a percentage of GNP (both in current prices).

Turner (1991, table 33, p. 92) finds that short-term bank flows are significantly correlated with the current account financing requirement with coefficients ranging from 0.27 (United Kingdom) to 0.88 (Canada) for seven of the ten OECD countries. In the case of FDI, however, Turner concludes that this flow is much closer to being autonomous than accommodating; the coefficient is significant only in the case of France with a value of only 0.13. Turner ranks long-term bank lending as the most autonomous, FDI next, portfolio investment third, and short-term bank loans as the most accommodative type of capital flow; Turner's results are reproduced here in Table 2. Only coefficients with t statistics of 1.5 and over are reported.

Using Turner's methodology with data on net capital flows from *International Financial Statistics* CD-ROM for a sample of sixteen developing countries,[4] I find a rather different response pattern, as shown in Table 3. In contrast to the OECD countries, other long-term capital flows appear to be just as sensitive to current account financing requirements as short-term flows in this sample of developing countries. For these countries, therefore, one might rank portfolio investment as the most autonomous, FDI or capital inflows to the public sector next, and both long- and short-term bank loans as the most accommodative type of capital flow.

All but one of the reported coefficients for FDI are less than 0.1; in Malaysia's case the coefficient is 0.14. On the basis of this table, therefore, FDI appears to be autonomous.[5] The negative coefficients of FDI in India, Korea, and the United Kingdom may reflect the deterrent effect of increasing current account deficits on FDI inflows, since large current account deficits can worsen a country's investment climate. This would also support the view that FDI inflows are largely unrelated to balance-of-payments financing requirements. However, it does suggest that FDI should be treated as endogenous to a country's saving-investment process.

Unfortunately, Turner's technique is seriously flawed. First, with enough substitutability between alternative forms of capital

---

[4]I drop Bermuda, China, Colombia, Hong Kong, Saudi Arabia, Singapore, and Taiwan from the developing countries listed in Table 1 on the basis of their small size or data deficiencies, but add India, Pakistan, and Sri Lanka.

[5]For the Southeast Asian developing economies, short-term bank loans seem slightly more accommodative than long-term loans, but the general pattern is similar to the pattern in the first part of the table.

TABLE 2

Sensitivity of Individual Capital Account Net Inflows to Current Account Financing Requirements in Ten OECD Countries, 1975–89

Country	Direct Investment	Portfolio Investment	Long-Term Flows	Short-Term Flows	Public Sector
United States				0.55 (2.8)	
Japan		0.51 (2.4)			0.20 (2.4)
Germany				0.30 (2.0)	
Canada		0.11 (1.6)		0.88 (3.1)	
France	0.13 (2.7)			0.32 (1.6)	
Italy				0.38 (2.7)	0.23 (2.2)
United Kingdom	–0.10 (–1.8)			0.27 (2.3)	0.25 (3.9)
Australia					0.36 (3.1)
Belgium-Luxembourg					0.22 (1.6)
Netherlands				0.47 (2.1)	

Note: *t* statistics are given in parentheses.
Source: Turner (1991), table 33, p. 92.

inflows, there may be no bivariate correlation between any of the components and the overall current account financing requirement. Indeed, this is the case for Egypt, Nigeria, and the Philippines in Table 3. Out of eighty regressions, only twelve yield

TABLE 3

Sensitivity of Individual Capital Account Net Inflows to Current Account Financing Requirements in Sixteen Developing Countries

Country	Direct Invest-ment	Portfolio Invest-ment	Long-Term Flows	Short-Term Flows	Public Sector
Argentina		0.14*			
(1975–89)		(2.2)			
Brazil			0.36**		
(1975–89)			(1.8)		
Chile			0.60**	0.66*	
(1975–91)			(2.0)	(3.5)	
Egypt					
(1975–88)					
India	−0.00*		0.35**		0.39**
(1975–89)	(−2.9)		(2.0)		(2.1)
Mexico	0.07**		0.41*	0.67*	
(1975–88)	(2.2)		(2.6)	(4.0)	
Nigeria					
(1975–90)					
Pakistan	0.05*				
(1975–90)	(2.9)				
Sri Lanka				0.21**	
(1975–91)				(2.0)	
Turkey		−0.09**		0.50*	
(1975–90)		(−2.1)		(2.9)	
Venezuela			0.62*		0.58*
(1975–91)			(2.5)		(2.5)
Indonesia	0.07*	0.05*			
(1975–90)	(2.2)	(3.3)			
Korea	−0.02**		0.32**	0.39**	
(1975–90)	(−2.0)		(1.8)	(2.1)	
Malaysia	0.14*				0.26**
(1975–90)	(2.5)				(1.8)
Philippines					
(1975–90)					
Thailand				0.38*	
(1975–90)				(3.2)	

Note: *t* statistics are given in parentheses. *95 per cent confidence level. **90 per cent confidence level.

significant coefficients at the 95 per cent confidence level. Second, the bivariate regressions fail to establish causality.

A country's current account deficit is financed by foreign saving. Just as national saving flows through several channels before reaching the investor, so too does foreign saving. One channel through which foreign saving flows is FDI. As Dooley (1990) points out, foreign direct investment constitutes a flow-of-funds concept and records a financial flow. Financial flows from saving to investment can take many forms, some of which are virtually perfect substitutes. For example, debt flows can become equity flows when tax reforms change incentives without affecting capital formation in any way. In the same way, foreign debt flows can become FDI flows without causing any change in capital formation. Because of the high degree of substitutability and fungibility in such financial flows, flow-of-funds data are seldom useful for economic analysis (Dooley 1990, p. 75). In other words, it may be difficult, if not impossible, to determine whether FDI is autonomous or accommodating, whether it increases capital formation or provides additional balance-of-payments financing, or whether it provides neither because an increase in FDI simply offsets a reduction in another type of capital flow. The evidence presented so far suggests that FDI does not provide additional balance-of-payments financing. Therefore, I now turn to the question of whether FDI increases capital formation or simply substitutes for other types of international capital flows.

4 Foreign Direct Investment in a Macroeconomic Model

WHETHER OR NOT SUBSTITUTABILITY and fungibility are so high that FDI flows provide no relevant economic information at all is an empirical question. The estimates of the current account financing requirement equation suggests that FDI is either a close substitute for at least one other type of capital flow or is indeed autonomous. In an attempt to discriminate between these two possibilities, I now investigate whether or not FDI affects the ratio of gross domestic investment to GNP. To do this, I use FDI as an explanatory variable rather than as the dependent variable in a five-equation macroeconomic model. Since causation could run both ways and FDI could well be determined simultaneously with saving and investment, I treat it as an endogenous variable.

Table 4 presents the macroeconomic model derived in this chapter; hats denote the endogenous variables. The extent and financing of a current account deficit depend both on a country's desire to spend more than its income and on the willingness of the rest of the world to finance the deficit from its saving. In other words, a current account deficit is determined simultaneously by both the demand for and the supply of foreign saving. My current account model attempts to capture the essential determinants of this interactive process. It also permits the ratio of foreign debt to GNP to converge to a constant and hence sustainable steady state (Fry 1989, 1993*b*). A steady state exists if a higher level

TABLE 4

A Macroeconomic Model of Foreign Direct Investment

$$IY = b_{10} + \overset{0/+}{b_{11}}\,\widehat{FDIY} + \overset{-}{b_{12}}\,FLY_{t-1} + \overset{+}{b_{13}}\,\widehat{DDCY} + \overset{-}{b_{14}}\,RW + \overset{?}{b_{15}}\,REXL_{t-1} + \overset{+}{b_{16}}\,\widehat{YG} + \overset{+}{b_{17}}\,YG_{t-1} + \overset{+}{b_{18}}\,IY_{t-1}. \tag{5}$$

$$SNY = b_{20} + \overset{0/-}{b_{21}}\,\widehat{FDIY} + \overset{?}{b_{22}}\,FLY_{t-1} + \overset{?}{b_{23}}\,RW + \overset{+}{b_{24}}\,\widehat{YG} + \overset{0/-}{b_{25}}\,(\widehat{YG}\cdot\widehat{FDIY}) + \overset{?}{b_{26}}\,(\widehat{YG}\cdot FLY_{t-1}) + \overset{?}{b_{27}}\,(\widehat{YG}\cdot RW) + \overset{+}{b_{28}}\,SNY_{t-1}. \tag{6}$$

$$IMKY = b_{30} + \overset{0/+}{b_{31}}\,\widehat{FDIY} + \overset{+}{b_{32}}\,\widehat{REXL} + \overset{+}{b_{33}}\,TTL + \overset{+}{b_{34}}\,\widehat{IKY} + \overset{+}{b_{35}}\,\widehat{XY} + \overset{0/+}{b_{36}}\,\widehat{OKY} + \overset{-}{b_{37}}\,FLY_{t-1} + \overset{0/+}{b_{38}}\,FDIY_{t-1} + \overset{0/+}{b_{39}}\,OKY_{t-1} + \overset{+}{b_{40}}\,IMKY_{t-1}. \tag{7}$$

$$XKY = b_{50} + \overset{0/+}{b_{51}}\,\widehat{FDIY} + \overset{+}{b_{52}}\,\widehat{REXL} + \overset{0/+}{b_{53}}\,\widehat{OKY} + \overset{0/+}{b_{54}}\,FDIY_{t-1} + \overset{0/+}{b_{55}}\,OKY_{t-1} + \overset{+}{b_{56}}\,IMKY_{t-1}. \tag{8}$$

$$YG = b_{60} + \overset{?}{b_{61}}\,\widehat{FDII} + \overset{+}{b_{62}}\,\widehat{IKY} + \overset{?}{b_{63}}\,\widehat{INF} + \overset{+}{b_{64}}\,\widehat{XKG}. \tag{9}$$

TABLE 4 (*Continued*)

		Endogenous Variables
IY	–	Domestic investment/GNP (current prices)
FDIY	–	Net inflow of foreign direct investment/GNP (dollar values converted to domestic currency, current prices)
DDCY	–	Change in domestic credit/GNP (current prices)
YG	–	Rate of growth in GNP (constant prices, continuously compounded)
SNY	–	National saving/GNP (current prices)
IMKY	–	Imports/GNP (constant prices)
REXL	–	Real exchange rate [(domestic GNP deflator/U.S. wholesale price index)/domestic currency per U.S. dollar]
IKY	–	Domestic investment/GNP (constant prices)
XY	–	Exports/GNP (current prices)
OKY	–	Other capital flows/GNP (dollar values converted to domestic currency, current prices)
XKY	–	Exports/GNP (constant prices)
FDII	–	Net inflow of foreign direct investment/domestic investment (dollar values converted to domestic currency, current prices)
XKG	–	Rate of growth in exports (constant prices, continuously compounded)
INF	–	Rate of change in GNP deflator (continuously compounded)
		Exogenous or Predetermined Variables
TTL	–	Terms of trade (export price index/import price index)
RW	–	World real interest rate (6-month LIBOR deposit rate minus U.S. inflation, continuously compounded)
FLY	–	Cumulated net foreign liabilities/GNP (dollar values converted to domestic currency, current prices)

of foreign indebtedness improves the current account.[6] If foreign indebtedness reduces investment by more than it reduces saving, or raises investment by less than it raises saving, rising foreign indebtedness improves the current account and so slows down the buildup of foreign debt.

[6]This constitutes an informal error-correction process.

FIGURE 1

Domestic Investment, National Saving, and the Current Account Deficit

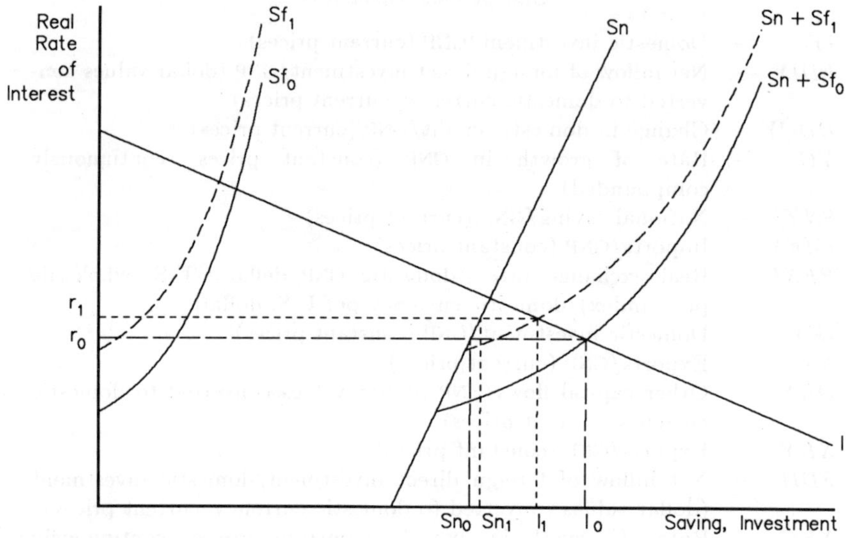

The key components of the model are represented in Figure 1. This figure echoes Metzler (1968) in viewing the current account deficit as the difference between domestic investment and national saving. It shows the planned levels of national saving, foreign saving, and domestic investment at different levels of inflation-adjusted or real interest rates. The domestic investment function I slopes downwards indicating that there is more investment at lower interest rates. The national saving function Sn is nearly vertical indicating that national saving does not vary greatly with changes in the domestic real interest rate.

Most developing countries face an upward-sloping supply curve of foreign saving Sf_0. However, the effective cost at which foreign saving begins to be supplied in any particular year depends on the country's foreign debt position inherited from past borrowing. In this model, the effective cost of foreign borrowing is also the effective domestic real interest rate. At an effective interest rate of r_0, domestic investment I_0 exceeds national saving Sn_0. Hence, the inflow of foreign saving is positive and the country runs a current account deficit on its balance of payments equal to $I_0 - Sn_0$.

The accumulation of foreign debt resulting from the current account deficit in year 0 raises the foreign saving curve to Sf_1. This change produces an effective cost of foreign borrowing of r_1 in year 1. In this case, foreign debt accumulation *reduces* domestic investment and *raises* national saving through a higher domestic real interest rate. As this process continues in subsequent years, the current account deficit declines until it reaches a steady-state equilibrium in which the foreign debt/GNP ratio is constant. Here then is an explanation for the positive effect of foreign debt on the U.S. current account detected by Masson, Kremers, and Horne (forthcoming) and Wickens and Uctum (forthcoming); higher foreign indebtedness eventually improves the current account and so reverses or reduces the foreign debt buildup. This is the stabilizing financial effect of foreign debt accumulation.

Much foreign debt in developing countries takes the form of government and government-guaranteed foreign debt. The level of this type of foreign debt accumulated from past current account deficits may itself affect the position of the saving function in Figure 1. Presumably, the modern Ricardian equivalence view would hold that if households expect the existence of government-guaranteed foreign loans to necessitate government expenditure and hence higher taxation in the future, private saving would rise as more guarantees were extended. Hence, the Ricardian equivalence hypothesis suggests that more foreign debt could actually raise the national saving ratio, since this *future* contingent government liability does not reduce the *current* level of government saving.

Alternatively, however, as households notice that government and government-guaranteed foreign debt is rising and anticipate higher future tax burdens for its servicing, they face an increasing incentive to transfer assets abroad, as foreseen by Ricardo:

> A country which has accumulated a large debt is placed in a most artificial situation; and although the amount of taxes, and the increased price of labour, may not, and I believe

> does not, place it under any other disadvantage with respect to foreign countries, except the unavoidable one of paying those taxes, yet it becomes the interest of every contributor to withdraw his shoulder from the burthen, and to shift this payment from himself to another; and the temptation to remove himself and his capital to another country, where he will be exempted from such burthens, becomes at last irresistible, and overcomes the natural reluctance which every man feels to quit the place of his birth, and the scene of his early associations. A country which has involved itself in the difficulties attending this artificial system, would act wisely by ransoming itself from them, at the sacrifice of any portion of its property which might be necessary to redeem its debt. (1817, p. 338)

Savers could also perceive that a high and rising foreign debt ratio may goad the government into stimulating exports, which would involve a devaluation in the real exchange rate. Indeed, a steady-state equilibrium necessitates a depreciation in the real exchange rate. In this case, the real returns on assets held abroad could be higher than the real returns on domestic assets. Hence, one might expect a higher value of foreign debt to reduce measured national saving, implying a leftward shift in the saving function in Figure 1.

The magnitude of capital flight caused by a buildup of foreign debt can be, and in several developing countries has been, destabilizing. Instead of an increase in foreign debt *reducing* domestic investment and *increasing* national saving, the foreign debt buildup shifts the national saving function to the left; hence, the current account deficit *increases.* Real interest rates can reach, and in several developing countries have reached, astronomical levels without reducing the current account deficit.

Indeed, in a number of developing countries, newly liberalized financial sectors subject to inadequate prudential supervision and regulation have magnified the impact of exogenous shocks by accommodating distress borrowing. In this way, banks in these countries compound the problem of insolvency in the real sectors of the economy. Because distress borrowers push real rates of interest to levels at which virtually no economic activity can be profitable, solvent businesses start to face a liquidity crunch which then forces them to borrow at rates which they know are unmanageable. The exceptionally high real interest rates produce an epidemic effect: the false credit demand by distress borrowers puts upward pressure on interest rates, which in turn drags down other firms. The supply of funds is made available because of explicit or implicit deposit insurance. Demand rises because of firms' expectations that government will bail out non-financial as well as financial enterprises. When net worth is zero, firms have every incentive to gamble on a government bailout in the future. In such conditions, foreign savings are scarce.

The end result is financial and economic paralysis. This then is the explanation of a *negative* effect of foreign debt on the current account; an increase in foreign debt can worsen the current account. This is the destabilizing fiscal effect of foreign debt accumulation which may or may not outweigh the stabilizing financial effect of foreign debt accumulation discussed above.

A country's foreign indebtedness can be estimated by cumulating the current account deficit over time; here one must use the balance-of-payments definition of the current account, which subtracts unrequited transfers from the measured deficit. The dollar stock of *net* foreign liabilities derived in this way can then be converted into domestic currency and expressed as a ratio of GNP. The variable representing these net foreign liabilities FLY_{t-1} is last year's stock of cumulated *net* foreign liabilities converted into domestic currency and divided by last year's GNP.

The main problem in estimating the model sketched in Figure 1 is that the effective cost of foreign borrowing or domestic shadow interest rate, r_0 and r_1 in Figure 1, is unobservable. As Hajivassiliou points out,

> The spread over the London interbank offer rate (LIBOR) does not perform the key role of clearing the market for international loans. Instead allocation of scarce credit among third world countries is fundamentally carried out through quantity offers and requests. (1987, p. 205)

Secondary market prices of developing country debt might provide an alternative measure of the opportunity cost of funds, but data exist only from 1985. To overcome this difficulty, a reduced-form equation for r can be derived from simple demand and supply functions for foreign saving. The demand for foreign saving equals the saving-investment gap, which depends on all the determinants of national saving and domestic investment, including the effective cost of foreign borrowing:

$$Sf^d = \xi(\overset{-}{r}).$$

The supply of foreign saving is determined by the world real interest rate RW plus a country-specific risk premium, the *effective* premium which produces the effective cost of foreign borrowing and hence the domestic shadow interest rate. This premium is determined, among other factors, by previous debt buildup FLY_{t-1} (Dooley 1986; Edwards 1986). Hence, the supply function can be expressed:

$$Sf^s = \zeta(\overset{+}{r}, \overset{-}{RW},\ \overset{-}{FLY}_{t-1}).$$

Equating demand and supply provides a reduced-form expression for the domestic shadow interest rate or the effective cost of foreign borrowing:

$$r = \varphi(\overset{+}{RW},\ \overset{+}{FLY}_{t-1}).$$

Hence, RW and FLY_{t-1} can be substituted for r in both investment and saving functions.

The Effect of Foreign Direct Investment on Domestic Investment

WHETHER OR NOT substitutability and fungibility are so high in the case of developing countries that FDI flows provide no relevant economic information is an empirical question. The estimates of current account financing requirements presented above suggest that FDI is either a close substitute for at least one other type of capital flow or is indeed autonomous. In an attempt to discriminate between these two possibilities, I now use FDI as an explanatory variable in an equation that explains the ratio of gross domestic investment to GNP IY. Since causation could run both ways and FDI could be determined simultaneously with saving and investment, I also treat it as an endogenous explanatory variable.

The investment function specified here in terms of the ratio of investment to GNP is based on the flexible accelerator model. Blejer and Khan (1984, pp. 382–83) describe some of the difficulties of estimating neoclassical investment functions for developing countries. Without data on the capital stock and the return to capital, there is little choice in practice but to use some version of the accelerator model.

The accelerator model has the desired capital stock K^* proportional to real output y:

$$K^* = \alpha y. \tag{10}$$

This can be expressed in terms of a desired ratio of net investment to output $(I/Y)^*$:

$$(I/Y)^* = \alpha\gamma, \tag{11}$$

where γ is the rate of growth in real output (denoted YG in the regression equation).

The partial adjustment mechanism specified for the investment *ratio* is somewhat more complicated than the equivalent mechanism for the *level* of investment. Specifically, there could be a lag in achieving the same investment ratio this year as last year if output rose rapidly last year; this year's desired investment *level* will be higher than last year's, despite a constant desired *ratio* of investment to output. To incorporate this adjustment lag, last year's growth rate γ_{t-1} can be included as an explanatory variable. In this case, however, the coefficient of γ_{t-1} was insignificant; hence γ_{t-1} is omitted from the estimate.

The remaining adjustment mechanism allows the actual investment rate to adjust partially in any one period to the difference between the desired investment rate and the investment rate in the previous period (λ is the coefficient of adjustment):

$$\Delta(I/Y) = \lambda[(I/Y)^* - (I/Y)_{t-1}] \tag{12}$$

or

$$I/Y = \lambda(I/Y)^* + (1-\lambda)(I/Y)_{t-1}. \tag{13}$$

The flexible accelerator model allows economic conditions to influence the adjustment coefficient λ. Specifically,

$$\lambda = \beta_0 + \left[\frac{\beta_1 z_1 + \beta_2 z_2 + \beta_3 z_3 + \cdots}{(I/Y)^* - (I/Y)_{t-1}} \right], \tag{14}$$

where z_i are the variables that affect λ. Since one of these variables can be an intercept term for the depreciation rate, the flexible accelerator model can be estimated for the gross rather than the net investment ratio.

A simple specification search suggests that, for the sixteen developing countries analysed here, the speed of adjustment is determined by the ratio of net FDI inflows to GNP *FDIY*, the lagged real exchange rate index expressed in natural logarithms $REXL_{t-1}$,[7] the lagged cumulated *net* foreign liabilities converted into domestic currency and divided by lagged GNP FLY_{t-1}, and credit availability as measured by the change in domestic credit divided by GNP *DDCY*.

The price of intermediate imports may affect the profitability of investment projects in these developing countries. Hence, the real exchange rate expressed in natural logarithms *REXL* is included as a proxy for the price of non-tradable goods in relation to import prices. I measure the real exchange rate *REX* as (domestic GNP deflator/U.S. wholesale price index)/domestic currency per U.S. dollar. Therefore, a higher value of *REXL* implies a lower relative price of imports. By appreciating the real exchange rate, capital inflows may stimulate investment. On the other hand, an appreciation in the real exchange rate prices exports out of world markets and may worsen the investment climate. Hence, its effect on investment is ambiguous.

Effective domestic costs of borrowing are extraordinarily difficult to measure in almost all developing countries because of selective credit policies and disequilibrium institutional interest rates; hence the quantity rather than the price of credit is used here. The availability of institutional credit can be an important

---

[7] The variable *REXL* is divided by 10 for scaling purposes in all the regression estimates.

determinant of the investment ratio, for the reasons
Blinder and Stiglitz (1983), Fry (1980), and Keller (1980).
specialize in acquiring information on default risk. Such information is highly specific to each client and difficult to sell. Hence, the market for bank loans is a customer market, in which borrowers and lenders are very imperfect substitutes. A credit squeeze rations out some bank borrowers who may be unable to find loans elsewhere and so be unable to finance their investment projects (Blinder and Stiglitz 1983, p. 300). Here, therefore, the investment ratio is influenced by the change in total domestic credit scaled by GNP *DDCY*.

Including FLY_{t-1} for the reasons discussed at the beginning of this chapter, the investment function derived from this flexible accelerator model for estimation purposes takes the form of equation 5 in Table 4. The dependent variable *IY* is gross domestic investment divided by GNP at current prices.

The Effect of Foreign Direct Investment on Saving

SO FAR, THE ANALYSIS of the effect of FDI on investment is incomplete in that it ignores possible effects of FDI on national saving and on the rate of economic growth. If FDI affects national saving directly or indirectly by influencing the rate of economic growth, its impact on the current account will not be identical to its impact on domestic investment. If FDI affects the rate of economic growth, it will also exert an indirect effect on domestic investment. In this and other ways, FDI could increase domestic investment by more than its own direct contribution.

My saving function *SNY* expressed as the ratio of national saving to GNP (both in current prices) is based on a life-cycle model (Mason 1987). The standard life-cycle saving model assumes that young, income-earning households save to finance consumption when they become old, non-earning households. Figure 2 illustrates these life-cycle patterns of income and consumption. Income $E(a)$ and consumption $C(a)$ of a household aged a are expressed as a fraction of lifetime income.

FIGURE 2

Life-Cycle Patterns of Income, Consumption, and Saving

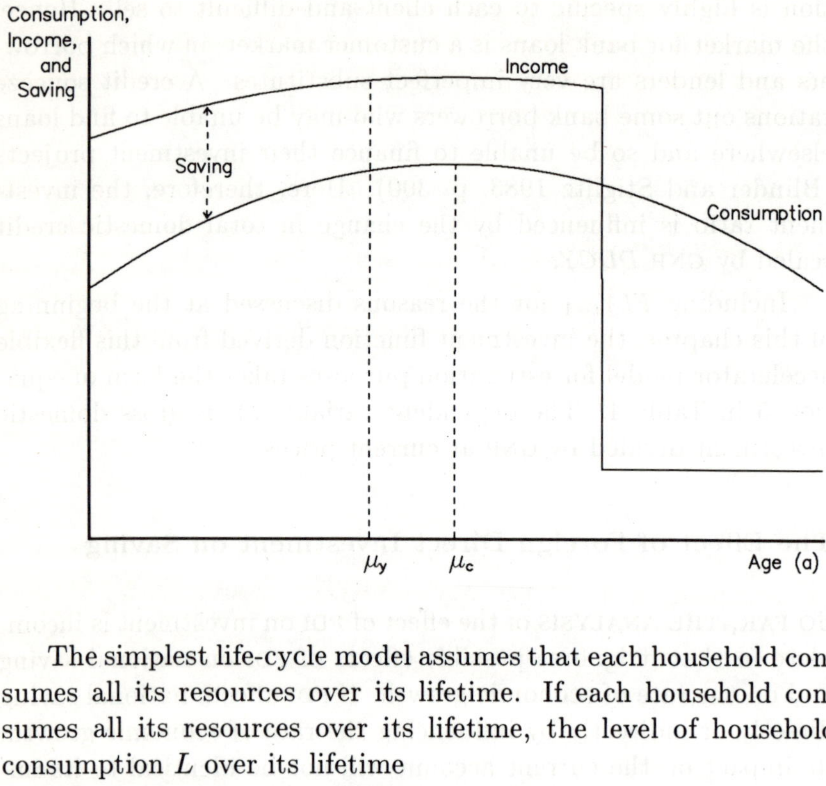

The simplest life-cycle model assumes that each household consumes all its resources over its lifetime. If each household consumes all its resources over its lifetime, the level of household consumption L over its lifetime

$$L = \int C(a)da \tag{15}$$

is equal to 1. Even if no household saves over its lifetime, this life-cycle model shows that aggregate saving can still be positive, provided that there is positive growth in aggregate real income. With positive growth, the lifetime resources of young savers exceed those of old dissavers and there will be positive aggregate saving. Because incomes of younger, earning households are higher than were incomes of older, non-earning households, saving exceeds dissaving in the society as a whole.

The aggregate saving ratio is determined by the age profile of the average household's saving $S(a) = E(a) - C(a)$ and by the lifetime resources that each age group can mobilize. If $V(a)$ is the ratio of lifetime resources of all households aged a to aggregate real income, then $V(a)S(a)$ is the total saving of age group a as a fraction of aggregate real income. The aggregate saving rate s is derived by summing across all age groups:

$$s = \int V(a)S(a)da. \tag{16}$$

With steady-state growth, $V(a)$ is independent of time and given by

$$V(a) = V(0)e^{-ga}, \tag{17}$$

where $V(0)$ is the ratio of lifetime resources of newly formed households to aggregate real income and g is the rate of growth in aggregate real income. If g is zero

$$s = V(0)(1 - L) = 0. \tag{18}$$

All aggregate real income is consumed because $V(a)$ is a constant, L equals 1, and $\int S(a)da$ is $1–L$.

With positive growth in aggregate real income, the lifetime resources $V(a)$ of young savers exceed those of old dissavers and there can be positive aggregate saving. This is the rate-of-growth effect. The rate-of-growth effect is itself determined by the relationship between income and consumption over the household's lifetime. Mason (1987) shows that the timing of household saving can be defined in terms of the mean ages of consumption μ_c and income μ_y, as shown in Figure 2. These are the average ages (weighted by the values of consumption expenditure and income at each age) at which half lifetime consumption and income are reached.

The higher is the rate of economic growth, the richer is the current generation compared with the previous generation. The rate-of-growth effect can be positive only to the extent that households on average accumulate wealth when they are younger in order to dispose of these assets when they are older. In countries where households can borrow against future income, households may have spent more than they have earned, in cumulative terms, for a large part of their lifetime. In this case, the rate-of-growth effect can be negative.

When the restrictive assumption of zero lifetime saving is discarded, the life-cycle model can incorporate both a level effect as well as the rate-of-growth effect discussed above. The level effect, which includes the bequest motive for saving, refers to the ratio of lifetime consumption to lifetime income. Any factor that increases this consumption ratio reduces the ratio of lifetime saving to lifetime income. It also reduces the ratio of current saving to current income.

The aggregate saving ratio can be represented approximately as a function of g, L, μ_c, and μ_y. All factors that influence the aggregate saving rate must enter through one of these four variables (Fry and Mason 1982, p. 430):

$$s \approx -\log(L) + (\mu_c - \mu_y)g. \tag{19}$$

Equation 19 allows factors that influence the timing of consumption or income over the life cycle to enter the saving function interactively with the rate of growth in income.

The level of household consumption can be approximated by a log-linear function in a vector of independent variables z:

$$L = e^{-\alpha z}. \tag{20}$$

The difference between the mean ages of consumption and income is represented by a linear function in the same vector of independent variables z:

$$\mu_c - \mu_y = \beta z. \tag{21}$$

Substituting equations 20 and 21 into equation 19 gives

$$s \approx \alpha z + \beta z g. \tag{22}$$

The world real interest rate RW is a determinant of the domestic real shadow interest rate and is also the return on foreign financial assets. Most developing countries prohibit capital outflows. Hence, much financial investment abroad takes place through overinvoicing imports and underinvoicing exports (Cuddington 1986, p. 38; Dooley 1986; Khan and Haque 1985; Watson et al. 1986).[8] This method of removing capital from a country reduces measured national saving, even if the true level of saving remains constant, because the national saving ratio is measured residually as the investment ratio plus the current account ratio ($SNY \equiv IY + CAY$, where SNY is national saving divided by GNP, IY is domestic investment divided by GNP, and CAY is the current account divided by GNP).

A higher world real interest rate could therefore reduce measured national saving, implying a leftward shift in the saving function in Figure 1.[9] Hence, a rise in RW could reduce measured saving, even if the substitution effect outweighs the income effect. In such case, the effect of a rise in the world real interest rate on the measured national saving ratio would be doubly ambiguous. In this study, the world real interest rate is proxied by the 6-month London Inter-Bank Offered Rate (LIBOR) on dollar deposits minus wholesale price inflation in the United States (both continuously compounded).

Inflows of FDI could also be accompanied by a decline in the measured national saving ratio. As in the case of a decline in measured national saving induced by an increase in the world real interest rate, the negative effect of FDI on national saving ratios may be a statistical artifact. If some residents realize that terms and conditions for FDI are more favourable than they are for locally financed investment, they have an incentive to remove capital from their country and to bring it back again in the form of FDI. To the extent that these individuals wish to conceal the capital

---

[8] An exporter submits an invoice for a smaller sum than that actually received for the exports when surrendering foreign exchange to the central bank; the difference can then be deposited in the exporter's bank account abroad. Conversely, an importer submits an invoice for an amount exceeding the true cost of the imports in order to siphon the difference into his foreign bank account.

[9] This saving function represents only that part of national saving available to finance domestic investment. Hence, it corresponds to measured national saving rather than the change in an individual's net worth.

outflow, they will also overinvoice imports and underinvoice exports. In such case, an increase in FDI would be accompanied by a reduction in recorded national saving (Fry 1993*a*). If this roundtrip capital flow does not occur, FDI would have no direct impact on the measured national saving ratio.

In effect, the saving function derived here is the private sector saving function Snp/Y to which the government saving ratio Sng/Y has been added; Snp is private national saving, Sng is government sector national saving, and Y is GNP. Unfortunately, disaggregated saving data are unavailable for most of the sample countries.[10] In any case, inflation badly distorts the measurement of disaggregated private and public saving because of the failure to account correctly for the inflation tax revenue. Fortunately, however, including components of public saving that are not substitutes for private saving affects only the intercept, provided they are independent of the explanatory variables (Fry and Mason 1982, p. 433).

Including FLY_{t-1} for the reasons discussed at the beginning of this chapter, the national saving function derived for estimation from this life-cycle model takes the form of equation 6 in Table 4. The dependent variable SNY is national saving divided by GNP at current prices. None of the interactive terms was significant and so they are omitted in the estimates reported in the next chapter. The lagged dependent variable is included to incorporate any adjustment lag.

The Effect of Foreign Direct Investment on Exports and Imports

IF FDI INCREASES DOMESTIC investment but has no effect on national saving, it worsens the current account. Equation 3 indicates that a change in the current account must be accompanied by an increase in imports, a decrease in exports, or by some

[10] Indeed, not even government deficit or government revenue and consumption expenditure data are available for many of the sample countries.

combination of increased imports and decreased exports. To investigate the trade effects of FDI inflows, I estimate both an import demand and an export supply function.

The import demand equation *IMKY* is expressed as the ratio of imports to GNP (both in constant prices). I assume that all the sample developing countries face an infinitely elastic supply of imports. Hence, their import volume is determined solely by their own demands. These demands are affected by the prices of exports, imports, and non-tradable goods. The price variables actually used here are the real exchange rate in natural logarithms *REXL*, as a proxy for the relative price of non-traded goods to imports, and the terms of trade in natural logarithms *TTL*,[11] which is of course the ratio of export to import prices.

The income elasticity of import demand is unitary,[12] but the composition of GNP affects imports. Specifically, investment is more import-intensive than consumption. Hence, the ratio of imports to GNP is determined in part by the ratio of investment to GNP (both in constant prices) *IKY*.

Adjustment to the desired level of imports may be constrained by the availability of foreign exchange earned by exporters. Many developing countries impose quantitative restrictions on imports of consumer goods. Typically, licences to import these restricted items are rationed not on the basis of total foreign exchange availability but rather on the availability of non-borrowed foreign exchange or foreign exchange earned by exporters. Both the ratio of nominal exports to nominal GNP *XY* and the lagged foreign debt ratio FLY_{t-1} are used to proxy rationing constraints. Since the coefficient of FLY_{t-1} was not significantly different from zero, this variable is omitted from the estimates reported below.

---

[11] The variable *TTL* is divided by 10 for scaling purposes in all the regression estimates.

[12] This is supported by the fact that the logarithm of per capita real GNP, the reciprocal of the logarithm of per capita real GNP, and the rate of economic growth are all insignificant in both the import demand and export supply functions.

Finally, *IMKY* may be influenced by FDI expressed as a ratio to GNP *FDIY* and by other capital inflows *OKY* also expressed as a ratio to GNP. In order to capture any delayed response to these capital inflows, I include current and lagged values of both variables. The import equation derived for estimation purposes takes the form of equation 7 in Table 4. Since neither the coefficient of lagged *FDIY* nor lagged *OKY* was significant in estimates that included and excluded the real exchange rate, these variables are omitted from the estimates reported in the next chapter.

An inflow of FDI could influence imports directly were it accompanied by an increase in imports for investment that would not have occurred in the absence of this FDI. In this case, FDI inflows are tied to the import of raw materials and capital equipment that would otherwise have not taken place. However, an inflow of FDI could also influence imports indirectly by appreciating the real exchange rate to stimulate unrelated imports and effect the transfer by increasing the current account deficit. For this reason, I estimate the import function with and without the real exchange rate *REXL* in order to test the extent to which FDI exerts an indirect rather than a direct effect on imports. If FDI is simply a substitute for other types of capital inflows, it would have no effect either directly or indirectly on imports.

In this model export supply *XKY*, expressed as the ratio of exports to GNP (both in constant prices), is determined by the relative prices of exports and non-traded goods *REXL* as well as by capital inflows *FDIY* and *OKY*. Hence, the export equation estimated here takes the form of equation 8 in Table 4.

Many developing countries impose a requirement that FDI be concentrated in their foreign trade sectors. Therefore, even if FDI has no impact on total domestic investment, it might change the composition of investment in a way that increased exports at some point in the future. Were the FDI concentrated in import-substitution activities, such a compositional shift could also decrease imports in the future. To test for these delayed effects of FDI on exports and imports, I estimate equations 7 and 8 with the average ratio of FDI to GNP over the previous five years *FDIYL* instead of the concurrent and 1-year lagged FDI ratio.

The Effect of Foreign Direct Investment on Economic Growth

BEFORE THE OVERALL effect of FDI on the current account can be determined, the effect of FDI on the rate of economic growth has to be analysed because growth affects both the domestic investment and national saving ratios. Lee, Rana, and Iwasaki (1986) estimate a simultaneous equation model of saving and growth for a sample of Asian developing countries. Of the various capital inflow components included in their growth rate equation, FDI has the greatest positive impact. The authors also find that FDI increases total factor productivity. Ishrat Husain and Jun (1992, p. 16) use a similar approach and also detect a significantly positive effect of FDI on the rate of economic growth for four ASEAN countries (Indonesia, Malaysia, Philippines, and Thailand).

The growth function specified as equation 9 in Table 4 has the rate of growth in GNP at constant prices *YG* affected positively by the investment ratio *IKY* and the rate of growth in exports *XKG* in constant prices. Inflation *INF* could stimulate growth in the short run through a Phillips curve effect. However, persistent inflation tends to reduce growth in the medium and long runs (Fry and Lilien 1986; Peng 1993).

A simple Harrod–Domar production function for a labour-surplus economy specifies output as a function of the capital stock with a constant incremental output/capital ratio σ. Taking first differences and dividing both sides by real GNP produces a function in which the rate of growth is determined by the investment ratio *IKY*. To determine whether FDI exerts a different effect on growth from domestically financed investment, that is, changes σ, I include the ratio of FDI to domestic investment *FDII*.[13]

Feder (1982) argues that there are two channels — higher marginal productivities and externalities — through which rapid export growth can affect the rate of economic growth in excess of the contribution of *net* export growth to GNP. If exports affect the production of non-exports with a constant elasticity θ, the rate

---

[13] I include *FDII* instead of *FDIY* to avoid multicollinearity with *IKY*.

of growth in *gross* exports at constant prices *XKG* captures solely the externality effect, while the rate of growth in exports scaled by the lagged export/GNP ratio *XKGY* picks up both the differential marginal productivity δ and the externality effects (Feder 1982, p. 67):

$$YG = \alpha \cdot FDIY + [\delta/(1+\delta) - \theta] \cdot XKGY + \theta \cdot XKG.$$

In fact, only *XKG* is significant for this country sample, implying that $\delta/(1+\delta) = \theta$.

Differential Effects of Foreign Direct Investment

CHAPTER 1 STRESSES THE point that FDI can take different forms in different countries. In some countries, FDI may augment capital formation, while in others it may represent a substitute capital flow or crowd out domestically financed investment. These different forms of FDI are likely to have different effects on a country's rate of economic growth. Hence, this chapter focuses on the effect of distortions in an economy on the productivity of FDI which, in turn, affects the rate of economic growth.

As the World Bank points out:

> Historically, the quality of investment has been at least as important for growth as the quantity. Although the fastest-growing countries had higher rates of investment than the others, empirical studies generally find that less than half the growth in output is attributable to increases in labor and capital. Higher productivity explains the rest. ... Faster growth, more investment, and greater financial depth all come partly from higher saving. In its own right, however, greater financial depth also contributes to growth by improving the productivity of investment. (1989, pp. 29–31)

An increasing body of evidence suggests that qualitative differences in investment are far more important than quantitative differences in explaining different rates of growth across countries (Fry 1988, chap. 6; King and Levine 1993; King and Levine forthcoming; Roubini and Sala-i-Martin 1992). These productivity differentials have been traced to trade distortions and financial repression imposed on the economy by government policy (Dollar 1992; Roubini and Sala-i-Martin 1991).

Trade distortions manifest themselves in a set of relative prices that deviate substantially from relative prices in the world economy. Relative prices in the economies of South Asia deviate considerably from relative world market prices. As the World Bank points out, "direct foreign investment in an economy with highly distorted policies is likely to generate net losses for the host country instead of welfare gains" (1991, p. 95). Indeed, the theory of immiserizing growth might well apply most forcefully in the case of FDI simply because FDI that produces negative value added at world prices can be accompanied by the removal of resources in the form of repatriated profits from the country.

The differential effects of FDI between countries can be examined in various ways. I use two alternatives here. First, I divide the sample into one group consisting of Southeast Asian developing economies (Indonesia, Korea, Malaysia, Philippines, and Thailand) and the remaining eleven countries in a control group. Second, I interact the FDI variable with factors that seem likely to affect its productivity. Specifically, I interact the FDI variable $FDIY$ with the black market exchange rate premium B used as a proxy for the degree of foreign exchange liberalization, the real rate of interest R (and R^2) as an indicator of the extent of financial repression or financial distortion, the degree of economic openness as measured by the average ratio of exports plus imports to GNP over the preceding five years TRL, the investment climate proxied by the average investment ratio over the preceding five years IYL, and the lagged foreign debt ratio FLY_{t-1}.

5 The Empirical Results

VIRTUALLY ALL THE EMPIRICAL investigations into the causes and consequences of FDI use single-equation models.[14] Here I estimate the five-equation macroeconomic model developed in Chapter 3 for a sample of sixteen developing countries (Argentina, Brazil, Chile, Egypt, India, Indonesia, Korea, Malaysia, Mexico, Nigeria, Pakistan, Philippines, Sri Lanka, Thailand, Turkey, and Venezuela). The results provide some new information on the direct and indirect effects of FDI inflows to this sample of developing countries. They also provide some strong indicators of the problems to be faced and pitfalls to be avoided by developing countries embarking upon policies to promote FDI inflows.

Foreign Direct Investment and Domestic Investment

THE REGRESSION METHOD used here is iterative three-stage least squares which is, asymptotically, full-information maximum likelihood (Johnston 1984, pp. 486–92). I estimate the sixteen individual country investment equations as a system of equations with cross-equation equality restrictions on all coefficients except the intercept. Hence, the estimates apply to a representative member

[14]The exceptions include the simultaneous two-equation models used by Lee, Rana, and Iwasaki (1986) and Ishrat Husain and Jun (1992).

of this sample of developing countries.[15] The estimation technique corrects for heteroscedasticity across country equations and exploits contemporaneously correlated disturbances. The instruments are the exogenous explanatory variables plus the lagged FDI ratio, lagged domestic credit expansion divided by GNP, the lagged terms-of-trade index in natural logarithms, lagged growth, the public sector borrowing requirement divided by GNP, the world real interest rate, oil price inflation, and the rate of growth (continuously compounded) in OECD output.[16] The estimation period is 1966–88 except for Brazil (1966–85), Chile (1966–84), Indonesia (1967–88), and Pakistan (1968–88).[17]

Table 5 gives three estimates of the investment function with the current FDI ratio and three estimates with the average FDI ratio over the previous five years *FDIYL* instead of the contemporaneous FDI ratio. For the complete sample, the foreign debt ratio reduces the domestic investment ratio, while the rate of economic growth increases it, as anticipated. The domestic credit variable is not significant in this estimate, while the negative coefficient of the real exchange rate suggests that an appreciation in the real exchange rate worsens the investment climate by pricing exports out of world markets. The coefficient of the lagged investment ratio indicates that 30 per cent of the adjustment to changes in the explanatory variables occurs in the current year. Hence, the effects of all the other explanatory variables on the domestic investment ratio are 3.3 times greater in the long run than they are in the short run.

The key coefficient, that of the ratio of net FDI inflows to GNP *FDIY*, is significantly negative for the sixteen sample developing countries as a group. The inflow of FDI could affect the investment ratio through its influence on the growth rate. When the growth

[15] The relevant coefficients in individual-country estimates were predominantly insignificant.

[16] The population growth rate is used as an instrumental variable for the growth rate estimates and current rather than lagged terms of trade is used in the trade equations.

[17] For the trade equations, the estimation period is 1965–88.

TABLE 5

Domestic Investment Estimates IY

Variable	All	Southeast Asia	Control
$\widehat{FDIY}$	–0.351	0.853	–0.738
	(–2.344)	(2.983)	(–3.398)
FLY_{t-1}	–0.049	–0.040	–0.024
	(–5.240)	(–2.592)	(–1.738)
$\widehat{DDCY}$	0.010	0.269	0.013
	(0.776)	(3.894)	(0.658)
$REXL_{t-1}$	–0.237	0.169	–0.198
	(–7.011)	(1.212)	(–3.651)
$\widehat{YG}$	0.255	0.330	0.219
	(14.482)	(4.853)	(6.803)
IY_{t-1}	0.703	0.679	0.753
	(30.576)	(12.766)	(21.093)
R^2	0.814	0.866	0.781
No. obs.	358	114	244
Investment with Lagged Foreign Direct Investment			
$FDIYL$	0.097	0.117	0.104
	(6.982)	(2.764)	(5.309)
FLY_{t-1}	–0.133	–0.139	–0.099
	(–10.393)	(–3.485)	(–5.751)
$\widehat{DDCY}$	0.039	0.241	0.011
	(3.277)	(3.427)	(0.623)
$REXL_{t-1}$	–0.111	–0.126	–0.207
	(–3.027)	(–0.836)	(–3.752)
$\widehat{YG}$	0.209	0.314	0.198
	(10.038)	(4.534)	(6.457)
IY_{t-1}	0.739	0.763	0.719
	(33.798)	(12.682)	(22.863)
R^2	0.832	0.858	0.798
No. obs.	355	115	240

Note: Hats denote endogenous variables, t statistics are given in parentheses.

rate is omitted, the FDI coefficients are slightly higher than the coefficients reported in Table 5 in all estimates. Hence, total direct and indirect effects of FDI on investment ratios are virtually identical to the direct effects shown in Table 5. The negative effect of FDI on the domestic investment ratio in these countries indicates that FDI neither increases domestic investment nor does it provide additional balance-of-payments financing.

Part of the problem may lie in the imposition of coefficient constraints across the entire country sample. Individual country estimates of the investment function indicate that the FDI coefficient is significant only in three countries. It is significantly negative in Chile but significantly positive in Indonesia and Malaysia. This would suggest a strategy of splitting the sample into subgroups. Hence, I estimate each equation for two subgroups — five Southeast Asian economies (Indonesia, Korea, Malaysia, Philippines, and Thailand) and a control group of the remaining eleven countries.

In Southeast Asia, FDI corresponds to capital formation on a one-to-one basis since the coefficient of *FDIY* is not significantly different from 1. This implies that FDI may not be a close substitute for other forms of capital inflow in these economies. Furthermore, it suggests that FDI does not crowd out or substitute for domestically financed investment. *Ceteris paribus,* it increases the current account deficit by the magnitude of the capital inflow. This conclusion that FDI is not a close substitute for other capital inflows in these Southeast Asian developing economies corroborates the same conclusion reached by Rana and Dowling (1990, p. 92) for a similar sample of Southeast Asian developing economies.

The Southeast Asian economies may differ from the control group because a number of Latin American countries have combined debt-equity swaps with programmes of privatization. In these cases, the deliberate aim of attracting FDI was not to increase capital formation but rather to substitute one form of capital inflow for another. The recorded net FDI inflow cancelled part of the country's foreign debt and was used to acquire holdings in the newly privatized industries such as Mexico's Teledyne. While this process of privatization continues, private investors may take a wait-and-see stance before undertaking new investment projects. Hence, the net inflow of FDI may be associated with a degree of uncertainty that clouds the investment outlook and so reduces capital formation.[18] This has not happened in Southeast Asia.

Use of FDI in debt-equity swap programmes may also have been a last resort measure taken under crisis conditions. Hence, the significantly negative coefficient for the control group may reflect the fact that FDI increased when the investment climate deteriorated in the wake of debt crises. In such case, the foreign debt crises may well have simultaneously reduced domestic investment and increased FDI. If so, higher FDI did not cause the decline in domestic investment but was associated with it since both were caused by some other factor.

The following estimate includes three interactive terms (356 observations):

$$\begin{aligned} IY = & -\underset{(-11.135)}{2.259}\,\widehat{FDIY} - \underset{(-3.303)}{1.411}\,\widehat{FDIY}\cdot B + \underset{(16.993)}{5.081}\,\widehat{FDIY}\cdot TRL \\ & -\underset{(-3.317)}{1.337}\,\widehat{FDIY}\cdot FLY_{t-1} - \underset{(-10.230)}{0.080}\,FLY_{t-1} + \underset{(6.473)}{0.057}\,\widehat{DDCY} \\ & -\underset{(-11.692)}{0.327}\,REXL_{t-1} + \underset{(28.825)}{0.315}\,\widehat{YG} + \underset{(33.408)}{0.610}\,IY_{t-1}. \end{aligned} \qquad (23)$$

$$R^2 = 0.806$$

In an attempt to pin down the key factors causing such disparate effects of FDI on domestic investment ratios across these two country groups, I interacted the black market exchange rate premium B, the real interest rate R, the degree of openness (the average ratio of exports plus imports to GNP over the preceding five years) TRL, the investment climate (the average investment ratio over the

[18] In some cases, however, the process of privatization appears to have improved the investment climate sufficiently to attract some complementary private capital inflows.

preceding five years) *IYL*, and the lagged foreign debt ratio FLY_{t-1} with the FDI ratio *FDIY*. Except for the real interest rate and the proxy for the investment climate, these variables produce significant interactive terms for the complete sample in equation 23.

Evidently, high black market exchange rate premiums and foreign debt ratios produce the negative association between FDI and the domestic investment ratio. If FDI constitutes a last-resort source of external financing during debt and balance-of-payments crises, it may well be associated with a reduction in investment productivity. In a direct test, I find that investment productivity does deteriorate as a country accumulates foreign debt (Fry 1989). In any event, an open economy with a low black market exchange rate premium (perhaps signifying open capital as well as current accounts) and a low foreign debt ratio experiences a positive association between FDI and the domestic investment ratio.

The bottom part of Table 5 presents estimates of the investment function with the average FDI ratio over the previous five years *FDIYL* instead of the contemporaneous FDI ratio. Evidently, lagged FDI is associated with higher domestic investment ratios. These estimates suggest that while FDI deters domestically financed investment in the current period, there is a small degree of intertemporal complementarity. In other words, past FDI stimulates current investment. The combination of contemporaneous substitutability and intertemporal complementarity is proposed by Molho (1986) in the context of firm holdings of real money balances and capital.

Foreign Direct Investment and National Saving

TABLE 6 GIVES THE NATIONAL saving function estimates. For the complete sample, increased foreign debt ratios reduce national saving ratios, as anticipated by Ricardo (1817, p. 338). However, since FLY_{t-1} reduces the national saving ratio by less than it reduces the domestic investment ratio, a rising debt ratio improves the current account and hence acts as a stabilizer. For each pair of foreign debt coefficients in the saving and investment equations,

TABLE 6

National Saving Estimates *SNY*

Variable	All	Southeast Asia	Control
$\widehat{FDIY}$	–0.650	–0.225	–0.237
	(–6.845)	(–0.691)	(–1.270)
FLY_{t-1}	–0.021	0.028	0.023
	(–3.651)	(1.820)	(2.514)
$\widehat{YG}$	0.155	0.379	0.090
	(8.420)	(5.968)	(2.931)
RW	0.122	0.011	0.077
	(3.509)	(0.126)	(1.533)
SNY_{t-1}	0.640	0.892	0.783
	(21.251)	(25.056)	(20.175)
R^2	0.858	0.847	0.847
No. obs.	364	114	250
Saving with Lagged Foreign Direct Investment			
$FDIYL$	0.052	–0.038	0.038
	(4.053)	(–0.998)	(1.505)
FLY_{t-1}	–0.033	0.058	–0.003
	(–2.925)	(1.702)	(–0.145)
$\widehat{YG}$	0.143	0.373	0.070
	(7.509)	(5.955)	(2.230)
RW	0.080	–0.014	0.102
	(1.821)	(–0.168)	(1.881)
SNY_{t-1}	0.798	0.888	0.781
	(37.067)	(25.534)	(20.097)
R^2	0.856	0.833	0.839
No. obs.	361	115	246

Note: Hats denote endogenous variables, t statistics are given in parentheses.

a rise in the foreign debt ratio increases saving by more than it increases investment, or reduces saving less than it reduces investment. Hence, for both subsamples a rise in the foreign debt ratio exerts a stabilizing influence on the current account.

A higher growth rate raises the national saving ratio as predicted by the life-cycle model. Higher world real interest rates also raise national saving ratios in this sample of countries. The coefficient of the lagged dependent variable indicates that about one-third of the adjustment occurs in the current year. Hence, the effects of all the other explanatory variables on the saving ratio are about three times greater in the long run than they are in the short run.

The estimate for the entire sample indicates that an increase in FDI reduces national saving.[19] Since its negative effect on the national saving ratio is larger than its negative effect on the domestic investment ratio, FDI inflows to these sixteen developing countries have a direct negative impact on the current account. When the growth rate is dropped from the saving estimates, the changes in the values of the FDI coefficients are minuscule. Hence, total direct and indirect effects of FDI on the current account are also negative.

The subsample estimates indicate that the control group is responsible for the negative effect of FDI on national saving for the whole sample. The coefficient of FDI in the Southeast Asia group estimate is not significantly different from zero.

As with the investment function, I interacted the black market exchange rate premium, the degree of openness, the investment climate, and the lagged foreign debt ratio with the FDI ratio in an attempt to detect any systematic influence of these variables on the relationship between FDI and saving behaviour. In this case, the degree of openness and the investment climate produce significant interactive term for the complete sample, but only when included in separate estimates (364 observations):

[19]The individual country estimates indicate that FDI inflows have significant impacts in only two countries; the coefficients are negative and significant in Chile and Korea.

$$SNY = -1.138\widehat{FDIY} + 0.869\widehat{FDIY} \cdot TRL - 0.016 FLY_{t-1} + 0.114 RW + 0.176\widehat{YG} + 0.653 SNY_{t-1}. \tag{24}$$

$$\begin{array}{cccccc} (-4.596) & (2.188) & (-2.895) & (3.268) & (10.426) & (22.297) \end{array}$$

$$R^2 = 0.862$$

In contrast to the results in the top half of Table 6, this approach suggests that a more open economy can anticipate a less negative effect of FDI on its national saving ratio. *Per se,* therefore, greater openness induces greater positive effects of FDI on both domestic investment and national saving ratios.

An improved investment climate also reduces the negative effect of FDI on national saving ratios, as shown in the following estimate for the complete sample (364 observations):

$$SNY = -2.126\widehat{FDIY} + 5.776\widehat{FDIY} \cdot IYL - 0.019 FLY_{t-1} + 0.096 RW + 0.197\widehat{YG} + 0.632 SNY_{t-1}. \tag{25}$$

$$\begin{array}{cccccc} (-6.892) & (4.900) & (-3.429) & (2.942) & (11.740) & (21.320) \end{array}$$

$$R^2 = 0.859$$

The bottom half of Table 6 gives three estimates of the national saving function with the lagged ratio of FDI. As with the investment function, lagged FDI has the reverse effect to current FDI on the national saving ratio. High FDI over the preceding five year period has a small but significant positive effect on national saving. One possible explanation is that a five-year period of high FDI inflows indicates improved stability of various kinds. Foreign investors have demonstrated confidence in the economy and the same confidence could reduce capital flight and so raise measured national saving.

TABLE 7

Export Estimates *XKY*

Variable	All	Southeast Asia	Control
$\widehat{FDIY}$	−0.337	0.543	−0.469
	(−2.981)	(1.625)	(−3.153)
$\widehat{OKY}$	−0.128	−0.241	−0.131
	(−10.983)	(−5.765)	(−8.421)
$\widehat{REXL}$	−0.025	−0.306	−0.083
	(−1.188)	(−2.210)	(−2.920)
XKY_{t-1}	0.953	1.018	0.885
	(65.176)	(47.328)	(33.745)
R^2	0.979	0.986	0.963
No. obs.	367	118	249
	Exports with Lagged Foreign Direct Investment		
FDIYL	0.026	0.080	0.010
	(5.166)	(3.105)	(1.593)
$\widehat{OKY}$	−0.129	−0.283	−0.107
	(−10.453)	(−6.995)	(−6.817)
$\widehat{REXL}$	−0.035	−0.075	−0.054
	(−1.293)	(−0.442)	(−1.736)
XKY_{t-1}	0.930	0.908	0.847
	(56.551)	(23.199)	(28.275)
R^2	0.980	0.986	0.964
No. obs.	362	117	245

Note: Hats denote endogenous variables, *t* statistics are given in parentheses.

Foreign Direct Investment and Trade Flows

TABLE 7 SHOWS THE EXPORT function estimates. I find that the coefficient of *FDIY* is virtually the same whether the real exchange rate *REXL* is included or excluded. This suggests that FDI does not affect exports indirectly through its impact on the real exchange rate. In the estimate for the complete sample, the coefficient of *FDIY* is significantly negative, suggesting that FDI may absorb domestically produced goods and services that would otherwise have been exported. However, this negative effect is not detected in Southeast Asia whether the real exchange rate is included or excluded from the equation.

In all estimates, the effect of other capital inflows *OKY* on exports is smaller than the effect of FDI. However, it exerts a negative effect on exports in all groups. This finding is consistent with the view that FDI is not an accommodating capital flow but that other capital flows are. Hence, a drop in exports produces a positive response from other capital flows. This is supported by the fact that the effect of other capital inflows does not change when the real exchange rate is omitted. In other words, other capital inflows do not appear to appreciate the real exchange rate and so do not reduce exports indirectly.

The real exchange rate itself exerts a negative influence on the ratio of exports to GNP because it raises the price of non-tradables relative to tradable goods. Producers find that domestic costs rise relative to their selling prices in world markets and so are deterred from export production. A rise in the real exchange rate encourages them to switch from export production into the production of non-tradable goods and services. However, this negative effect is significant only for the Southeast Asian subgroup.

The bottom half of Table 7 shows the export function estimates with the average FDI ratio over the previous five years *FDIYL*. The results here are entirely different from those shown in the top half of Table 7. Far from reducing exports, FDI which has taken place over the past five years increases exports significantly in all three groups. The estimates reported in the bottom half of Table 7 suggest that FDI has been directed successfully towards export-oriented activities. Given that FDI does not increase aggregate domestic investment (Table 5), FDI must change the composition of aggregate domestic investment. In other words, FDI crowds out domestically financed investment in other sectors. Table 6 suggests that some of this crowding out may be a result of roundtrip capital flows. Residents may remove capital from their country which would otherwise have financed non-export oriented investments and brought it back to finance investments in the export

sector. That FDI leads to a higher export ratio is explained in part by the fact that many developing countries impose performance criteria on FDI inflows, some of which relate to export performance. However, although significant, the effects of FDI over the previous five years on current exports is extremely small.

Table 8 shows the import function estimates. These estimates show that import ratios are increased by other capital inflows as well as by an appreciation in the real exchange rate, but that they are decreased by a deterioration in the terms of trade.[20] The investment ratio exerts a strong positive impact on the import ratio, as does the ratio of export earnings to GNP. The coefficient of the lagged import ratio indicates that about half the adjustment occurs in the current year. Hence, the magnitudes of the effects of all the other explanatory variables on the saving ratio in the long run are about twice their short-run magnitudes. All the coefficients in the import function accord with *a priori* expectations.

In fact, both sets of import equation estimates show only one substantial difference between the estimate for the entire sample and the estimates for the subsamples; the lagged FDI variable exerts a negative effect in the whole sample and in the control group, but a positive effect in Southeast Asia. As in the case of the export estimates, the import estimates without the real exchange rate *REXL* show no significant increase in the impact of FDI. Hence, FDI does not appear to raise imports indirectly by appreciating the exchange rate. Indeed, the FDI coefficient of 1 in the estimate for the complete sample suggests that FDI is accompanied by additional imports of equal value.

The bottom half of Table 8 shows the import function estimates with five-year lagged FDI. These estimates indicate that FDI has been directed successfully towards import-substitution activities as well as to export industries, except in Southeast Asia. In Southeast Asia, lagged FDI has a significantly positive impact on imports, suggesting that FDI has financed production of goods requiring imported raw materials and semi-processed goods. The

[20]The issue of simultaneity between capital flows and imports is addressed by treating capital flows as endogenous and using instrumental variables.

TABLE 8

Import Estimates *IMKY*

Variable	All	Southeast Asia	Control
$\widehat{FDIY}$	1.028	1.279	0.696
	(10.513)	(5.175)	(4.553)
$\widehat{OKY}$	0.144	0.209	0.123
	(12.057)	(4.548)	(7.163)
$\widehat{REXL}$	0.714	0.838	0.318
	(18.896)	(5.163)	(7.506)
TTL	–0.037	–0.024	0.014
	(–1.498)	(–0.319)	(0.459)
$\widehat{IKY}$	0.175	0.069	0.098
	(11.128)	(1.578)	(5.077)
$\widehat{XY}$	0.228	0.264	0.119
	(15.637)	(7.164)	(4.852)
$IMKY_{t-1}$	0.489	0.503	0.625
	(24.921)	(10.582)	(19.175)
R^2	0.972	0.969	0.968
No. obs.	366	118	248
Imports with Lagged Foreign Direct Investment			
$FDIYL$	–0.033	0.071	–0.050
	(–3.994)	(3.778)	(–4.784)
$\widehat{OKY}$	0.131	0.171	0.124
	(10.859)	(3.741)	(9.027)
$\widehat{REXL}$	0.647	0.503	0.174
	(16.248)	(3.631)	(4.476)
TTL	–0.120	0.097	0.016
	(–4.614)	(1.125)	(0.648)
$\widehat{IKY}$	0.231	0.099	0.090
	(13.333)	(2.064)	(5.012)
$\widehat{XY}$	0.268	0.206	0.100
	(16.696)	(4.858)	(4.594)
$IMKY_{t-1}$	0.453	0.553	0.531
	(20.902)	(11.199)	(13.754)
R^2	0.972	0.967	0.969
No. obs.	361	117	244

Note: Hats denote endogenous variables, t statistics are given in parentheses.

fact that Southeast Asian economies are generally not resource rich supports this interpretation. In all three groups, the impact of lagged FDI on exports exceeds its impact on imports; hence lagged FDI improves the current account. Nevertheless, the effects of FDI over the previous five years on exports, imports (whether positive or negative), and the current account are extremely small in all three country groups.

Foreign Direct Investment and the Rate of Economic Growth

ESTIMATES OF THE RATE of growth in real GNP *YG* for the sample developing countries are shown in Table 9. Export growth exerts a small positive effect on the growth rate, while higher inflation reduces growth except in Southeast Asia. The FDI variable in this equation is the ratio of FDI to domestic investment *FDII* which is substituted for *FDIY* to avoid multicollinearity with *IKY*. The variable *IKY* includes both domestically financed as well as foreign direct investment; it is aggregate capital formation in the economy. Hence, an insignificant coefficient of *FDII* indicates that FDI does not exert a significantly different effect from domestically financed investment on the rate of economic growth. In the control group, the significantly negative coefficient implies that growth falls when *FDII* rises.

The bottom half of Table 9 substitutes the average FDI ratio over the preceding five years for the ratio of FDI to domestic investment. A sustained period of high FDI inflows is associated with higher economic growth. As in the case of the positive effect of lagged FDI on the national saving ratio, perhaps a five-year period of high FDI inflows indicates improved stability which in turn improves efficiency of resource allocation. It might also reflect lagged demonstration effects and other externalities from FDI on current total factor productivity growth.

Although Table 9 suggests that the direct effects of current and lagged FDI ratios on rates of economic growth do not vary across the country groups, I tested a variety of effects interacted with

TABLE 9
Rate of Growth Estimates *YG*

Variable	All	Southeast Asia	Control
$\widehat{FDII}$	0.010	0.101	–0.126
	(0.419)	(1.805)	(–2.159)
$\widehat{IKY}$	0.239	0.142	0.250
	(23.184)	(8.745)	(20.095)
$\widehat{INF}$	–0.025	0.092	–0.032
	(–4.254)	(4.285)	(–4.601)
$\widehat{XKG}$	0.051	0.162	0.049
	(4.123)	(5.627)	(2.453)
R^2	0.164	0.133	0.150
No. obs.	355	114	241
Growth with Lagged Foreign Direct Investment			
FDIYL	0.036	0.039	0.020
	(6.030)	(1.705)	(1.760)
$\widehat{IKY}$	0.210	0.157	0.223
	(24.100)	(9.360)	(11.282)
$\widehat{INF}$	–0.042	–0.008	–0.030
	(–9.182)	(–0.715)	(–4.460)
$\widehat{XKG}$	0.042	0.184	0.023
	(3.677)	(6.531)	(1.170)
R^2	0.179	0.170	0.155
No. obs.	351	115	236

Note: Hats denote endogenous variables, *t* statistics are given in parentheses.

both the FDI variable and with the investment ratio. The first significant interactive term is between the lagged FDI variable and the investment ratio (351 observations):

$$\begin{aligned} YG = {} & \underset{(24.182)}{0.213\widehat{IKY}} + \underset{(5.382)}{0.137\widehat{IKY} \cdot FDIYL} \\ & - \underset{(-8.478)}{0.037\widehat{INF}} + \underset{(3.403)}{0.039\widehat{XKG}} \\ & R^2 = 0.169 \end{aligned} \tag{26}$$

This positive effect of lagged FDI on investment productivity may again reflect spillovers from previous FDI on the efficiency of current investment.[21] Of course, a high and stable inflow of FDI over a five-year period itself reflects a country's macroeconomic management, foreign trade and exchange rate policies, and other factors likely to improve investment efficiency.

One estimate of a function in which growth is determined solely by the FDI ratio, the real interest rate, and the export growth rate interacts the real interest rate with FDI in level, quadratic, and cubic form. This permits the real interest rate to exert a nonlinear effect on FDI efficiency. For the sixteen-country sample, the iterative three-stage least-squares estimate is (297 observations):

$$\begin{aligned} YG = {} & \underset{(7.599)}{0.582\widehat{FDIY}} + \underset{(17.134)}{0.093R} \\ & - \underset{(-12.621)}{9.425(\widehat{FDIY \cdot R})} - \underset{(-6.082)}{5.965(\widehat{FDIY \cdot R^2})} \\ & + \underset{(5.647)}{2.886(\widehat{FDIY \cdot R^3})} + \underset{(13.142)}{0.065\widehat{XKG}}. \\ & R^2 = 0.161 \end{aligned} \tag{27}$$

[21] However, Aitken and Harrison (1992) and Haddad and Harrison (1992) do not detect spillovers from FDI to domestically financed investment in the same industries in their microeconomic estimates of the effects of capital formation owned by foreign firms.

A similar relationship is produced when the investment ratio is used instead of the FDI ratio. Initially, I estimated an equation of the form:

$$YG = \beta_1(IKY) + \beta_2[IKY \cdot (R + \beta_3) \cdot (R + \beta_3)] + \beta_4(XKG).$$

Since the parameter β_3 was not significantly different from zero, although its negative value implies that growth is maximized at some positive real interest rate, I drop it from the estimate reported here (297 observations):

$$\begin{aligned} YG = {} & 0.164\widehat{IKY} - 0.237(\widehat{IKY} \cdot R^2) + 0.070\widehat{XKG}. \\ & (11.541) \qquad (-5.123) \qquad\qquad (12.628) \\ & R^2 = 0.217 \end{aligned} \tag{28}$$

Estimates that included both the investment ratio and FDI as a proportion of domestic investment interacted with R^2 failed to converge.

I derive this functional form from a claim by De Gregorio and Guidotti (1992) that real interest rates are not a good indicator of financial repression or distortion. Appealing to work by Calvo and Coricelli (1992), they suggest that the relationship between real interest rates and economic growth might resemble an inverted U:

> Very low (and negative) real interest rates tend to cause financial disintermediation and hence tend to reduce growth, as implied by the McKinnon–Shaw hypothesis. ... On the other hand, very high real interest rates that do not reflect improved efficiency of investment, but rather a lack of credibility of economic policy or various forms of country risk, are likely to results in a lower level of investment as well as a concentration in excessively risky projects. (De Gregorio and Guidotti 1992, p. 9)

For this reason, De Gregorio and Guidotti abandon real interest rates in favour of domestic credit to the private sector divided by GNP.

In fact, the point made by Calvo and Coricelli (1992) and De Gregorio and Guidotti (1992) holds up well in this growth rate estimate. The overall effect of a rising real interest rate on growth

FIGURE 3

Effect of Real Interest Rate on Economic Growth Rate

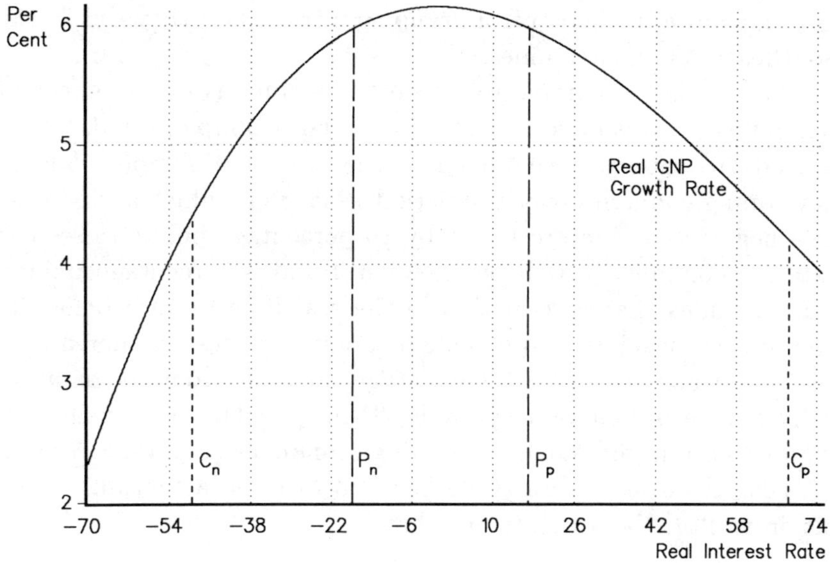

in equation 27 is illustrated in Figure 3. This figure is produced using the mean values of all the explanatory variables with the exception of the real deposit rate of interest. The mean value of the real deposit rate is zero with a standard deviation of 23 per cent. Its minimum value is –83 per cent and its maximum value 221 per cent. Figure 3 shows that the relationship between the real interest rate and growth does indeed resemble an inverted U. Both very low and very high real interest rates reduce growth both directly and through the effects of such interest rates on FDI productivity.

The line P_n denotes two standard deviations below the mean of all negative interest rates in the Southeast Asian economies, C_n denotes two standard deviations below the mean of all negative interest rates in the remaining eleven countries (the control group), P_p denotes two standard deviations above the mean of all zero or positive interest rates in the Southeast Asian economies, while C_p denotes two standard deviations above the mean of all zero or positive interest rates in the control group countries. Evidently, real interest rates deviated from their growth-maximizing level far more in the control group countries than they did in the Southeast Asian economies.

This result is comparable to other estimates of the effect of real interest rates of economic growth. For example, Polak (1989, pp. 66–70) reports econometric estimates for a sample of forty developing countries over the period 1965–85 in which an increase in a negative real interest rate by 10 percentage points raises the rate of economic growth by between 2 and 3 percentage points. He concludes that a reduction in the real interest rate below its equilibrium level by 1 percentage point requires an increase in the investment ratio by 1 percentage point in order to maintain a fixed rate of economic growth. I find similar relationships in various samples of Asian developing economies (Fry 1988, 1991).

Distortion in foreign trade has also received attention. In relation to FDI, Naya points out that

> the immiserization literature is of great significance because it illustrates how FDI and other capital flows can lead to suboptimal welfare levels, and even reduce welfare below pre-flow levels, when recipient industries are protected. In short, since protection will result in non-optimal investment decisions by foreign investors which in turn cause a misallocation of resources, the level of social welfare could easily be lower with foreign investment in a protected industry than without it. (1990, p. 298)

The indicator used here is the black market foreign exchange premium B because of its availability on an annual basis for all sixteen sample countries (353 observations):

$$YG = \underset{(1.941)}{0.274\widehat{FDIY}} - \underset{(-2.879)}{1.331}(\widehat{FDIY} \cdot B^2) + \underset{(2.410)}{0.029\widehat{XKG}}. \tag{29}$$

$$R^2 = 0.175$$

The effect of a rise in the black market foreign exchange premium is illustrated in Figure 4. The growth rate is reduced as the black

FIGURE 4
Effect of Black Market Exchange Rate Premium on Economic Growth Rate

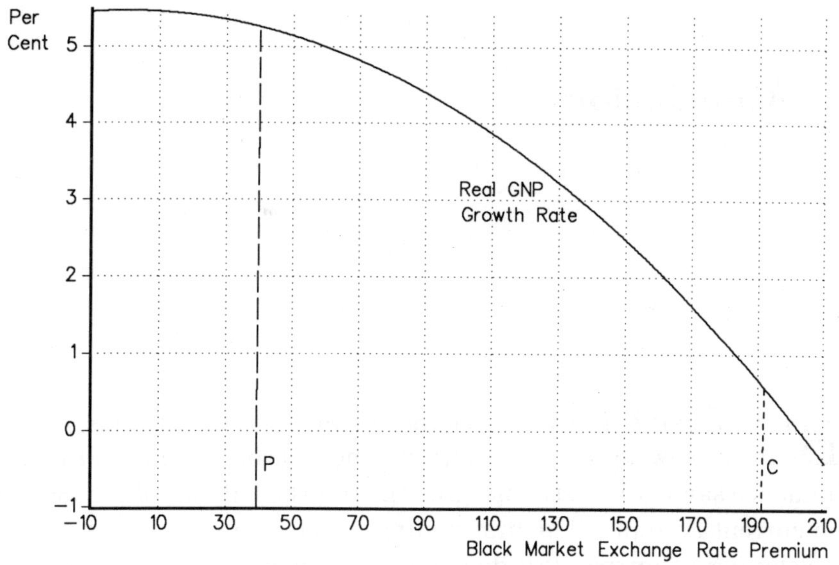

market exchange rate premium rises through its effect on FDI productivity. The mean value of the black market exchange rate premium is 31 per cent with a standard deviation of 63 per cent. Its minimum value is –10 and its maximum value is 639 per cent.

The line *P* denotes two standard deviations above the mean of all zero or positive black market exchange rate premia in the Southeast Asian economies, while *C* denotes two standard deviations above the mean of all zero or positive black market exchange rate premia in the control group of countries. Evidently, black market exchange rate premia tended to be considerably higher in the control group than they were in the Southeast Asian economies.

6 Conclusion

By analysing FDI in a macroeconomic framework, this study throws new light on various channels through which FDI can influence saving, investment, growth, and the balance of payments on current account. The first finding is that in a sample of sixteen developing countries, FDI does not provide additional balance-of-payments financing for a pre-existing current account deficit. In the eleven developing countries constituting a control group, FDI is associated with reduced domestic investment, so implying that FDI to these countries is simply a close substitute for other capital inflows. For five Southeast Asian developing market economies, however, FDI raises domestic investment by the full extent of the FDI inflow. In these countries, therefore, FDI has not been used as a substitute for other types of capital inflows but has increased capital formation and so worsened the current account.

In examining some secondary effects, I find that FDI has a significantly negative impact on national saving in this sample of developing countries. For the control group, this negative effect is of similar magnitude to the negative effect of FDI on domestic investment, implying a zero effect on the current account. However, the negative effect of FDI on national saving in the five Southeast Asian developing market economies indicates that FDI could have a negative effect on the current account in excess of its negative effect through increased domestic investment.

I also find distinctive differences in the effects of FDI on economic growth in the control group and the Southeast Asian developing market economies. While FDI has a negative effect on growth in the first country group, it has the same positive effect on growth as domestically financed investment in the latter country group.

Finally, for the complete sample of sixteen developing countries, I show that FDI raises the rate of economic growth in the absence of financial repression and trade distortions. However, financial repression as measured by the real deposit rate of interest and trade distortions as measured by the black market exchange rate premium can both cause FDI to be immiserizing.

The overall conclusion of this study is that both the nature and the effects of FDI flows vary significantly between different regions of the developing world. Outside Southeast Asia, FDI appears to have been used in large part as a substitute for other types of foreign flows; it has not increased aggregate domestic investment. When the control group countries attracted more FDI inflows, national saving, domestic investment, and the rate of economic growth all declined. Hence, FDI appears to have been immiserizing in these countries. In contrast, the role of FDI in Southeast Asia has been benign. In these economies, FDI financial flows have not been close substitutes for other types of foreign capital flows.

The superior efficiency of FDI in the Southeast Asian economies reflects not only less distorted financial conditions than in other parts of the developing world but also less distorted trading systems. The outward orientation of the Southeast Asian economies ensures that relative prices cannot diverge too far from world market prices. Under these conditions, there are few possibilities for FDI to find high profits in protected markets.

The favourable investment climates in the developing economies of Southeast Asia have ensured that FDI flows are readily available without the need for governments to discriminate in favour of this particular form of investment finance. Hence, these economies have avoided the two major pitfalls of FDI, namely, low or negative productivity caused by distortions in the economy and expensive discriminatory incentives provided in the mistaken belief that FDI brings externalities.[22]

Recently, Goldstein, Mathieson, and Lane have noted the links between macroeconomic policies that promote domestic saving and capital repatriation on the one hand, and a successful experience with FDI on the other hand:

> At a minimum, domestic fiscal, monetary, exchange rate, and financial policies must be designed to create stable domestic economic and financial market conditions, to provide domestic residents with clear incentives to hold their savings in domestic financial claims, and to ensure that available domestic and foreign savings are used to support productive investment. Stable economic conditions are also important for encouraging foreign direct investment. (1991, p. 43)

It comes as no surprise, therefore, to find a strong positive correlation between the ratio of domestically financed investment to GNP and the ratio of FDI to GNP.

Indeed, inflows of foreign direct and portfolio investment provide good indicators of development performance and potential. Policies aimed directly at stimulating these forms of capital inflows appear to be ineffective or to produce the opposite effects to those desired. The evidence suggests overwhelmingly that policies that promote domestic investment and growth are most likely to stimulate private sector capital inflows in all forms. In summarizing findings similar to those of Balasubramanyam (1984), Agarwal, Gubitz, and Nunnenkamp conclude:

> . . . the effectiveness of tax and tariff exemptions as well as related privileges for FDI, some of which are very costly for the host countries, is uncertain at best. They may even result in a vicious circle if privileges granted to foreign investors give rise to hostile feelings against FDI in the recipient countries. The consequences may be a new wave of regulations,

[22]The Maxwell Stamp report (1991, p. 246) concludes that general economic conditions can outweigh various deterrents such as poor accounting standards: "foreign investors in Thailand do not appear to have been discouraged by these factors".

TABLE 10

Direct Effects of Foreign Direct Investment Inflows

Variable	All	Southeast Asia	Control
Domestic investment	neg.	≈ 1	neg.
National saving	neg.	n.s.	n.s.
Exports	neg.	n.s.	neg.
Imports	≈ 1	≈ 1	pos.
Economic growth	n.s.	n.s.	n.s.
Domestic investment (lagged FDI)	pos.	pos.	pos.
National saving (lagged FDI)	pos.	n.s.	n.s.
Economic growth (lagged FDI)	pos.	n.s.	n.s.
Exports (lagged FDI)	pos.	pos.	n.s.
Imports (lagged FDI)	neg.	pos.	neg.

Note: n.s.: not significantly different from zero at the 95 per cent confidence level.

> intensified efforts to circumvent the restrictions, and finally the retreat of foreign investors. It appears more promising to adhere to the rule: "what is good policy for domestic investors is also good for foreign investors", by creating a stable and favourable general framework for investment. Ad hoc interventions should be kept to the minimum. It is not only the rules and regulations that matter, but also how they are applied in practice. The approval procedure should be fast and transparent as it is a crucial element in the investment decision of foreign companies. (1991, p. 128)

The evidence presented in this chapter is certainly consistent with this conclusion.

By analysing FDI in a macroeconomic framework, this study throws new light on various channels through which FDI can influence saving, investment, growth, and the balance of payments on current account. Table 10 sets out the direct effects of larger FDI inflows in the three groups of developing economies examined in this study. The first empirical finding for a sample of sixteen developing countries is that FDI does not provide additional balance-of-payments financing for a pre-existing current account deficit. Since FDI is associated with reduced domestic investment outside Southeast Asia, this implies that FDI is a close substitute for other capital inflows and may also crowd out domestically financed investment. In Southeast Asia, however, FDI raises domestic investment by the full extent of the FDI inflow. In these countries, therefore, FDI has not been used as a substitute for other types of capital inflows but has increased capital formation and so worsened the current account. Furthermore, in these countries FDI has not crowded out domestically financed investment. By increasing domestic investment in these economies, FDI has increased growth rates.

In examining some other effects, I find that FDI has a significantly negative impact on national saving in this sample of developing countries. One possible explanation is that residents may find that terms and conditions for FDI are more favourable than they are for locally financed investment. Hence, they would have an incentive to remove capital from their country and to bring it back again in the form of FDI. To the extent that these individuals wish to conceal the capital outflow, they will overinvoice imports and underinvoice exports. In such case, an increase in FDI would be accompanied by a reduction in recorded national saving.

The concurrent effect of FDI on exports is negative outside Southeast Asia. One possible explanation is that FDI accommodates export declines in the control countries. In contrast, however, FDI inflows over the preceding five years are associated with higher export ratios. Given the earlier finding that FDI does not increase aggregate domestic investment outside Southeast Asia, the strong positive effect of lagged FDI inflows on exports may be caused by a change in the composition of investment. In other words, FDI may crowd out, at least in part, domestically financed investment in countries outside Southeast Asia. Unsurprisingly, the investment financed by FDI seems to be export-oriented.

An inflow of FDI is strongly associated with a higher import ratio. The immediate effect of FDI, therefore, is to finance a larger import bill. However, FDI inflows over the preceding five years are associated with a significant decline in the import ratio outside Southeast Asia. In these control countries, FDI seems to have been directed not only into export industries but also into import-substitution activities. In all three country groups, higher lagged FDI inflows improve the current account. In the control group, FDI inflows over the preceding five years raise exports and reduce imports.

Finally, I show that FDI raises the rate of economic growth in the absence of financial repression and trade distortions in the sixteen sample developing countries taken together. However, financial repression as measured by the real deposit rate of interest and trade distortions as measured by the black market exchange rate premium can both cause FDI to be immiserizing. When the domestic economy is distorted, FDI inflows are associated with a low or negative growth. When real interest rates are positive, however, FDI can accelerate the rate of economic growth more when restrictions on the sectoral location of this investment are relaxed.

The policy implications that might be derived for developing countries about to embark upon policies to attract FDI are:

- Foreign direct investment can increase capital formation or provide additional balance-of-payments financing but cannot perform both functions at the same time. If FDI is attracted for privatization or debt-equity swap programmes, it may provide additional or alternative balance-of-payments support, but it will not accelerate capital formation or economic growth.

- Stimulating FDI through special incentive schemes may simply encourage roundtrip capital flows from the host country. In such case, measured national saving may fall.

- In the presence of financial and trade distortions, FDI can remove from the host country more than it contributes. In other words, it can be immiserizing.

- The most efficacious way of encouraging FDI is to implement policies that generally improve the investment climate. Where domestically financed investment is booming, FDI will seek to participate. Nondiscrimination discourages roundtrip capital flows and reduces the possibilities for immiserization.

- Maximum benefit from FDI can be achieved in open economies that are free of domestic distortions such as financial repression and trade controls. Under such conditions, restrictions on the sectoral location of FDI reduce its growth-enhancing impact.

References

Agarwal, Jamuna P., Andrea Gubitz, and Peter Nunnenkamp. *Foreign Direct Investment in Developing Countries: The Case of Germany.* Kieler Studien 238. Tubingen: JCB Mohr (Paul Siebeck), 1991.

Aghevli, Bijan B., James M. Boughton, Peter J. Montiel, Delano Villanueva, and Geoffrey Woglom. *The Role of National Saving in the World Economy: Recent Trends and Prospects.* Occasional Paper 67. Washington, D.C.: International Monetary Fund, March 1990.

Aitken, Brian and Ann Harrison. "Does Proximity to Foreign Firms Induce Technology Spillovers? Evidence from Panel Data". Cambridge, Mass.: Massachusetts Institute of Technology, July 1992.

Balasubramanyam, Venkataraman N. "Incentives and Disincentives for Foreign Direct Investment in Less Developed Countries". *Weltwirtschaftliches Archiv* 120, no. 4 (1984): 720–35.

Blejer, Mario I. and Mohsin S. Khan. "Government Policy and Private Investment in Developing Countries". *International Monetary Fund Staff Papers* 31, no. 2 (June 1984): 379–403.

Blinder, Alan S. and Joseph E. Stiglitz. "Money, Credit Constraints, and Economic Activity". *American Economic Review* 73, no. 2 (May 1983): 297–302.

Calvo, Guillermo A. and Fabrizio Coricelli. "Stagflationary Effects of Stabilization Programs in Reforming Socialist Countries: Enterprise-Side vs. Household-Side Factors". *World Bank Economic Review* 6, no. 1 (January 1992): 71–90.

Cockcroft, Laurence and Roger C. Riddell. "Foreign Direct Investment in Sub-Saharan Africa". International Economics Department, WPS 619. Washington, D.C.: World Bank, March 1991.

Cuddington, John T. "Capital Flight: Estimates, Issues, and Explanations". *Princeton Studies in International Finance,* no. 58 (December 1986).

De Gregorio, José and Pablo E. Guidotti. "Financial Development and Economic Growth". WP/92/101. Washington, D.C.: International Monetary Fund, December 1992.

Dollar, David. "Outward-Oriented Developing Economies Really Do Grow More Rapidly: Evidence from 95 LDCs, 1976–1985". *Economic Development and Cultural Change* 40, no. 3 (April 1992): 523–44.

Dooley, Michael P. "Country-Specific Risk Premiums, Capital Flight and Net Investment Income Payments in Selected Developing Countries". DM/86/17. Washington, D.C.: International Monetary Fund, March 1986.

———. "Comment". In *Taxation in the Global Economy,* edited by Assaf Razin and Joel Slemrod, pp. 74–78. Chicago: University of Chicago Press for the National Bureau of Economic Research, 1990.

Dornbusch, Rudiger and Park Yung Chul. "Korean Growth Policy". *Brookings Papers on Economic Activity,* no. 2 (1987), pp. 389–444.

Edwards, Sebastián. "The Pricing of Bonds and Bank Loans in International Markets: An Empirical Analysis of Developing Countries' Foreign Borrowing". *European Economic Review* 30, no. 3 (1986): 565–89.

Faini, Riccardo and Jaime de Melo. "Adjustment, Investment and the Real Exchange Rate in Developing Countries". *Economic Policy: A European Forum,* no. 11 (October 1990): 491–519.

Feder, Gershon. "On Exports and Economic Growth". *Journal of Development Economics* 12, no. 1 (February–April 1982): 59–73.

Fry, Maxwell J. "Money, Interest, Inflation and Growth in Turkey". *Journal of Monetary Economics* 6, no. 4 (October 1980): 535–45.

———. *Money, Interest, and Banking in Economic Development.* Baltimore: Johns Hopkins University Press, 1988.

———. "Foreign Debt Instability: An Analysis of National Saving and Domestic Investment Responses to Foreign Debt Accumulation in 28 Developing Countries". *Journal of International Money and Finance* 8, no. 3 (September 1989): 315–44.

———. "Domestic Resource Mobilization in Developing Asia: Four Policy Issues". *Asian Development Review* 9, no. 1 (1991): 15–39.

———. "Saving, Investment and Current Account Imbalances: A Malaysian and East Asian Perspective". International Finance Group, IFGWP–93–05. Mimeographed. Birmingham: University of Birmingham, July 1993*a*.

———. "Foreign Debt Accumulation: Financial and Fiscal Effects and Monetary Policy Reactions in Developing Countries". *Journal of International Money and Finance* 12, no. 4 (August 1993*b*): 347–67.

Fry, Maxwell J. and David M. Lilien. "Monetary Policy Responses to Exogenous Shocks". *American Economic Review, Papers and Proceedings* 76, no. 2 (May 1986): 79–83.

Fry, Maxwell J. and Andrew Mason. "The Variable Rate-of-Growth Effect in the Life Cycle Saving Model: Children, Capital Inflows, Interest and Growth in a New Specification of the Life-Cycle Model Applied to Seven Asian Developing Countries". *Economic Inquiry* 20, no. 3 (July 1982): 426–42.

Goldstein, Morris, Donald J. Mathieson, and Timothy Lane. "Determinants and Systemic Consequences of International Capital Flows". In *Determinants and Systemic Consequences of International Capital Flows,* edited by Research Department of the International Monetary Fund, pp. 1–45. Occasional Paper No. 77. Washington, D.C.: International Monetary Fund, March 1991.

Guisinger, Stephen E. "Do Performance Requirements and Incentives Work?" *World Economy* 9, no. 1 (March 1986): 79–96.

Haddad, Mona and Ann Harrison. "Are There Positive Spillovers from Direct Foreign Investment? Evidence from Panel Data for Morocco". Mimeographed. Washington, D.C.: World Bank, May 1992.

Hajivassiliou, Vassilis A. "The External Debt Repayments Problems of LDCs: An Econometric Model Based on Panel Data". *Journal of Econometrics* 36, nos. 1–2 (September–October 1987): 205–30.

Hill, Hal. "Foreign Investment and East Asian Economic Development". *Asian-Pacific Economic Literature* 4, no. 2 (September 1990): 21–58.

Ishrat Husain and Jun Kwang W. "Capital Flows to South Asian and ASEAN Countries". Mimeographed. International Economics Department, WPS 842. Washington, D.C.: World Bank, January 1992.

International Monetary Fund. *International Financial Statistics Yearbook.* Washington, D.C.: International Monetary Fund, various issues.

Johnston, John. *Econometric Methods.* 3rd ed. New York: McGraw–Hill, 1984.

Keller, Peter M. "Implications of Credit Policies for Output and the Balance of Payments". *International Monetary Fund Staff Papers* 27, no. 3 (September 1980): 451–77.

Khan, Mohsin S. and Nadeem Ul Haque. "Foreign Borrowing and Capital Flight: A Formal Analysis". *International Monetary Fund Staff Papers* 32, no. 4 (December 1985): 606–28.

King, Robert G. and Ross Levine. "Finance and Growth: Schumpeter Might Be Right". *Quarterly Journal of Economics* 108, no. 3 (August 1993): 717–37.

———. "Finance, Entrepreneurship, and Growth: Theory and Evidence". *Journal of Monetary Economics* 32 (forthcoming).

Lee Jungsoo, Pradumna B. Rana, and Yoshihiro Iwasaki. "Effects of Foreign Capital Inflows on Developing Countries in Asia". Economic Staff Paper No. 30. Mimeographed. Manila: Asian Development Bank, April 1986.

Mason, Andrew. "National Saving Rates and Population Growth: A New Model and New Evidence". In *Population Growth and Economic Development: Issues and Evidence,* edited by D. Gale Johnson and Ronald D. Lee, pp. 523–60. Madison: University of Wisconsin Press for the National Academy of Sciences, 1987.

Masson, Paul, Jeroen Kremers, and Jocelyn Horne. "Net Foreign Assets and International Adjustment: The United States, Japan, and Germany". *Journal of International Money and Finance* 13, no. 1 (forthcoming).

Maxwell Stamp Ltd. *Regional Study of Resource Flows and Financial Intermediation.* London: Maxwell Stamp, October 1991.

Meade, James E. *The Theory of International Economic Policy. Volume 1: The Balance of Payments.* Oxford: Oxford University Press, 1951.

Metzler, Lloyd A. "The Process of International Adjustment under Conditions of Full Employment: A Keynesian View". In *Readings in International Economics,* edited by Richard E. Caves and Harry G. Johnson, pp. 465–86. Homewood, Ill.: Richard D. Irwin for the American Economic Association, 1968.

Molho, Lazaros E. "Interest Rates, Saving, and Investment in Developing Countries: A Re-Examination of the McKinnon–Shaw Hypothesis". *International Monetary Fund Staff Papers* 33, no. 1 (March 1986): 90–116.

Naya, Seiji. "Direct Foreign Investment and Trade in East and Southeast Asia". In *The Political Economy of International Trade: Essays in Honor of Robert E. Baldwin,* edited by Ronald W. Jones and Anne O. Krueger, pp. 288–312. Cambridge, Mass.: Basil Blackwell, 1990.

Organisation for Economic Co-operation and Development. *Investment Incentives and Disincentives: Effects on International Direct Investment.* Paris: Organisation for Economic Co-operation and Development, 1989.

Peng WenSheng. "The Effects of Inflation on Natural Output Growth in Six Pacific Basin and Latin American Developing Economies". International Finance Group, IFGWP–93–02. Mimeographed. Birmingham: University of Birmingham, April 1993.

Polak, Jacques J. *Financial Policies and Development.* Paris: Development Centre of the Organisation for Economic Co-operation and Development, 1989.

Rana, Pradumna B. and J. Malcolm Dowling. "Foreign Capital and Asian Economic Growth". *Asian Development Review* 8, no. 2 (1990): 77–102.

Ricardo, David. *On the Principles of Political Economy, and Taxation.* London: John Murray, 1817.

Roubini, Nouriel and Xavier Sala-i-Martin. "Financial Development, the Trade Regime, and Economic Growth". NBER Working Paper No. 3876. Mimeographed. Cambridge, Mass.: National Bureau of Economic Research, October 1991.

———. "Financial Repression and Economic Growth". *Journal of Development Economics* 39, no. 1 (July 1992): 5–30.

Turner, Philip. *Capital Flows in the 1980s: A Survey of Major Trends.* Monetary and Economic Department, BIS Economic Papers No. 30. Basel: Bank for International Settlements, 1991.

United Nations. *World Investment Report 1992: Transnational Corporations as Engines of Growth.* New York: United Nations, 1992.

Watson, C. Maxwell, G. Russell Kincaid, Caroline Atkinson, Eliot Kalter, and David Folkerts-Landau. *International Capital Markets: Developments and Prospects.* World Economic and Financial Surveys. Washington, D.C.: International Monetary Fund, December 1986.

Wickens, Michael and Merih Uctum. "The Sustainability of Current Account Deficits: A Test of the US Intertemporal Budget Constraint". *Journal of Economic Dynamics and Control* 17 (forthcoming).

World Bank. *World Development Report 1989.* New York: Oxford University Press for the World Bank, 1989.

———. *World Development Report 1991.* New York: Oxford University Press for the World Bank, 1991.

THE AUTHOR

MAXWELL J. FRY holds the Tokai Bank Chair in International Finance at the University of Birmingham. His previous positions include the London School of Economics, the University of Hawaii, the University of California at Irvine and Los Angeles, Oxford University, and consultancies with the Asian Development Bank, the Bank of England, the International Monetary Fund, the Organisation for Economic Co-operation and Development, and the World Bank. Since 1970, the author has published extensively on financial aspects of economic development, including articles in the *American Economic Review, Economic Journal,* and *Journal of Political Economy,* as well as ten books. *Money, Interest, and Banking in Economic Development* (1988) has been translated into Arabic, Chinese, and Spanish; a second edition is scheduled for 1994.